RULES OF THUMB

BY TOM PARKER

2

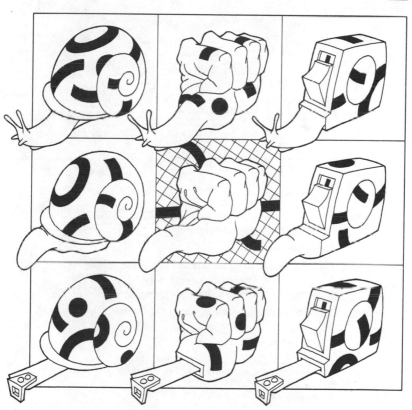

HOUGHTON MIFFLIN COMPANY BOSTON
1987

Other books by Tom Parker

Rules of Thumb
In One Day

Library of Congress Cataloging-in-Publication Data

Parker, Tom.
  Rules of thumb 2.

  Includes index.
  1. Handbooks, vade-mecums, etc.   I. Title.
AG106.P37   1987   031'.02   87-3097
ISBN 0-395-42955-2 (pbk.)

Printed in the United States of America

BTA .11,10 9 8 7 6 5 4 3 2

To Pete and Carol Ayer, Wisconsin's finest

THANKS

Rule of thumb: If you want something done, ask a busy person to do it.

First of all, thanks to Cally Arthur. She's got plenty to do, yet she helped, more than anyone, to pull this collection together.

Thanks, again, to Cheryl Russell, who continues to come to my rescue, even though she's a lot busier than I am.

Thanks to Kat Dalton, busy designer, for finding the time to work on this book.

Thanks to Walter Pitkin for his special help and advice. And thanks again to Gerard Van der Leun for pushing this project out of the nest five years ago. Also, I'd like to thank the busy staff and readers of *The Whole Earth Review*; they've been pitching in from the start.

Three cheers for Jon Crispin, Dede Hatch, and Jon Reis, the busy photographers featured in this book. Based in Ithaca, New York, their work is widely shown and appears in such impressive places as the *New York Times*, *Business Week*, *Progressive Architecture*, *Time*, and *Newsweek*. All three are busy because they're so good.

And obviously, this book is mostly the work of the busy people who took the time to send in their favorite rules of thumb. Their names accompany their contributions, but a few people deserve special mention. Scott Parker (no relation) ran away with the prize for number of rules submitted. His contributions, which came by audio cassette with hard-copy backup, put Beaumont, Texas, on the map. I'd also like to thank Rick Eckstrom, Michael Rider, Ned Frederick, Andrea Frankel, Phil Schrodt, Dean Sheridan, Peter Reimuller, L. M. Boyd, and Dirck Z. Meengs. I love those fat letters.

And finally, thanks to Gerry M. Flick, ship's surgeon, and the rest of the crew of the S.S. *Constitution*. I enjoyed your postcards and I know you must be busy on that cruise ship off the coast of Hawaii. No really, I mean it.

CALL FOR ENTRIES

Rules of thumb don't die, they accumulate. As the collection grows, new rules hatch themselves. They update each other. They reflect the cleverness of their times. Imagine a book with ten or even twenty thousand rules of thumb — the first encyclopedia for know-it-alls. If you have a rule of thumb you would like to add to our file,* mail it to:

RULES OF THUMB
P.O. Box 6680
Ithaca, New York 14851

*The fine print: If your rule of thumb is used, Houghton Mifflin will credit you as the source, but there will be no compensation beyond instant immortality.

INTRODUCTION

Y ou know what a rule of thumb is, right? A rule of thumb is a homemade recipe for making a guess. It is an easy-to-remember guide that falls somewhere between a mathematical formula and a shot in the dark.

Timothy Wenk, a magician from West Stockbridge, Massachusetts, has conjured up a trick for looking good on stage: He buys a suit that costs four times his fee for one performance. That's a rule of thumb.

Joan Isbell is not a magician, but she has a rule of thumb too: The distance between an alligator's eyes, in inches, is its length, in feet. When Joan sees two alligator eyes floating sixteen inches apart on the surface of a pond, her rule of thumb tells her not to swim between them.

A rule of thumb is a tool. Pull a good one out of your hat and — abracadabra — you turn information you have into information you need.

I collect rules of thumb. A few years ago when I published my favorites in a book called *Rules of Thumb*, I asked readers to send me more.

The new rules came in waves. One day my mailbox would be stuffed with oddball postcards and strange-looking letters, then nothing for several days. I thought I was seeing some sort of complicated feedback cycle as people passed the book around. A neighbor of mine who likes to gripe about our mom-and-pop post office — it's in the back of someone's house — had a different theory: He said they'd bring me a new batch of rules whenever they finished reading them.

If they were reading carefully, the people at my post office would know how to avoid lunatics on city buses and how to win a duel with pistols (aim at the knees). Sometimes I watched as the letter carrier pulled up to the mailbox in her rusty barge of a car. I wonder how she felt about delivering postcards that said, "A rotten egg will float" or "A sex change operation will age you five years." I'll bet she was thrilled to learn that when Americans talk, they stand just far enough apart to reach out and stick their fingers into each other's ears.

Maybe someday I'll set up a rules of thumb test facility. You know, people in lab coats with clipboards and stuff like that. I received one letter suggesting that any burglar could improve his or her chances of success by taking along a fresh steak to feed the guard dog. Now that would be fun to test. I could grab a slab of meat, pad myself with two weeks of dirty laundry, and head for the nearest junkyard full of guard dogs. Would a nasty dog really bite someone who just tossed him a prime rib? And do all junkyards really have dogs? What if I met the owner instead? I wonder if that piece of meat would stop a load of shotgun pellets.

You have in your hands the best rules of thumb I've collected since book number one. Each rule is followed by a source, or rumored source, or the name of the first person who sent it to me. The people listed are not necessarily claiming a rule of thumb as their own invention. A lot of contributors sent in rules they heard from someone else. Many sent clippings or paraphrased another source. Some rules arrived as hearsay. Don't feel cheated if your mother's rule of thumb was sent in by an Italian psychologist from Nashville — your mother's rule is getting famous.

Frankly, I can't say that all of these rules of thumb work. Some would be pretty hard to test. How would you check the rule that says one elephant will provide as much meat as one hundred antelopes?

There were lots of submissions I threw out. One said simply, "Monday is the windiest day of the week." Sure it is.

Aaron "Airbag" Simpson, of the University of North Carolina, said, "Never kick a woman out of bed for eating crackers unless she wants to mess around on the floor." Come on, Airbag, you should be studying.

Or how about this one? "My rule of thumb is that the leader of the rock band Stone Poneys catapulted ten feet into the audience when his electric guitar got a short in it." Huh?

There were weird ones too, like the one written in crayon and signed "Ronald, age 38." Those aren't included here. They look best stuck on my refrigerator door.

I'm not saying I tossed out everything I should have. I like to be flexible. There was only one rule of thumb from Nebraska, so I wasn't about to throw that out. And sometimes the actual rule is less interesting than the person who sent it in. Why would Rob Shapiro, a charter pilot, have a rule of thumb for making tofu from soybeans?

Other rules are just plain curious. Emery Nemethy, of Catawissa, Pennsylvania, sent me this rule of thumb: "On rainy nights, 90 percent of the worms crossing a highway will be facing the same direction." It may be a while before I need to use his rule of thumb, but I like to think of Emery out alone on a warm, wet Pennsylvania night, bent over a patch of flashlight, counting worms in the drizzle.

Then there's Emmon Bodfish, of Oakland, California. Emmon figures that, as a rule of thumb, a relaxed person needs to inhale twelve times every minute. Emmon's research also shows that it takes two minutes for the sun to drop out of sight after it first touches the horizon. These are not earthshaking rules, but it's nice to think of Emmon just sitting on his porch swing, counting breaths and watching the sun go down. Emmon's rules stayed in.

Some rules depend on where you live. A rule of thumb for planting beans in Georgia might put you out of business in New York. If Emmon Bodfish was sitting on his porch swing in Nome, Alaska, instead of Oakland, he would have to wait months, not minutes, for the sun to go down.

So the rules of thumb collection continues to grow. Give this batch a try. If a certain rule doesn't work for you, invent your own version. If it still doesn't work, write and tell me about it. That's what Lola Marcel of Cleveland, Oklahoma, did. I know she's been doing her homework:

Dear Mr. Parker:

In regard to your book "Rules of Thumb," I would like to know where you got your information on the fact that your wedding ring size is the same as your hat size. My wedding ring size is 5 and my hat size is 6¾ and my husband's wedding ring size is 9 and his hat size is 7¼, so your fact is wrong.

Don't you do research before you write a book? If you don't, I think you better start. Plus I think your publishers should check your facts before they publish a book for you. Needless to say, I would not pay any amount for this particular book.

> An interested reader,
> Mrs. Lola Marcel
> Cleveland, Oklahoma

Do I need any more proof that a rule of thumb is a highly personal thing? Consider this book a treasury of private inventions that work for the people who sent them in. So immortalize yourself: Write down your own rule of thumb and drop it in the mail. My post office will pass it along as soon as they're done with it.

And thanks for the letter, Lola. The rules of thumb archive stands corrected. Heck, I probably shouldn't admit it, but I always thought Cleveland was in Ohio.

To determine the proper wattage for an aquarium heater, allow three watts per gallon in a room at normal temperature. Use four watts per gallon for a room that is cooler than normal.

Mary Ellen Parker, teacher, Cincinnati, Ohio

1. CATCHING A BANK ROBBER   Suspects fleeing the scene of a crime in a car will make right turns more often than left because they don't want to waste valuable time waiting for cross traffic to clear. If you didn't see which way they went, try turning right.   *John Howsden, police sergeant, Fremont, California*

2. THE SLINKY RULE   Never buy more than one Slinky because they eventually will become intertwined.
Andy Steinberg, Louisville, Kentucky

3. PLANNING A MASSAGE   It takes ninety minutes to give a full body massage, plus an additional five minutes for each bad joke the client tells before the session. The number of bad jokes is directly proportional to the thickness of a person's body armor.   *Geanne Toma, massage therapist, Lebanon, New Hampshire*

4. WRITING A POEM   When you're writing a poem, eliminate nine out of ten adjectives and adverbs in the first draft, and cut everything you've heard before.
Jennifer Welch, poet and editor, Columbus, Ohio

5. WAKING UP WITH A CAT   Generally speaking, if your cat nudges your feet in the morning, it wants to stay inside. If it nudges your face, it wants to go out.
Mark McMullen, accountant, Alexandria, Virginia

6. PICKING YOUR RASPBERRIES   When you start to find garden spiders in your raspberries, you have one week left to pick.   *Carol Ayer, raspberry grower, West Bend, Wisconsin*

7. DECIDING WHICH INVITATIONS TO ACCEPT   Accept all invitations, even to occasions you won't look forward to, because half of all social arrangements fall through and you will get credit for being friendly. If you end up attending a few things against your will, don't worry. You'll be surprised to find yourself enjoying more than half of those.
Lucy Cummin, stay-at-home, Huntington, Vermont

8. MAKING FRIENDS WITH A DOG   If you want to be friends with somebody else's dog, let the dog make the first move, and don't be too quick to respond.
Walter Pitkin, literary agent, Weston, Connecticut

9. WEIGHING YOUR SALARY   If a single career woman is not making her age times $1,000 in annual salary by age thirty, she should either change careers or marry a career man making $80,000 or better and become a wife and mother. She can then live comfortably and afford one additional child for each $20,000 per year he makes over $80,000.
Barbara Greenlee, B.S., R.N., ship's nurse, Kauai, Hawaii

The distance between an alligator's eyes, in inches, is its length, in feet.
Joan Isbell, horticulturist, Ithaca, New York

JON REIS

10. CHECKING FOR NERVE DAMAGE   Skin with damaged nerves doesn't wrinkle in warm water.   *Scott Parker, Beaumont, Texas*

11. BUYING OCEANSIDE PROPERTY   If you are north of the equator, don't buy property on the south side of a jetty. The drift of the ocean is from south to north, and the beach will erode south of any protrusion that blocks the drift.
Carol Terrizzi, artist and graphic designer, Ithaca, New York

12. BOILING AN EGG   The hymn "Onward, Christian Soldiers," sung in a not-too-brisk tempo, makes a good egg-timer. If you put the egg into boiling water and sing all five verses, with the chorus, the egg will be just right when you come to "amen."
Mrs. G. H. Moore, London, England, quoted in The New Yorker

13. FIRING A SALUTE   Repeating "If I wasn't a gunner, I wouldn't be here" will give you the two-second interval between rifle salutes.   *John Fountain, Riverside, Connecticut*

14. CHARCOALING CHICKEN   If you're going to barbecue chickens for a large group of people, you'll need one pound of charcoal per whole chicken.
John Van Der Mark, city fireman, Ithaca, New York

15. FOLLOWING WORMS   On rainy nights, 90 percent of the worms crossing a highway will be facing the same direction.
Emery Nemethy, Catawissa, Pennsylvania

16. CHOOSING BETWEEN TWO THINGS   If you can't decide between two alternatives — let's say, between a blue suit and a gray one — toss a coin (heads, it's blue; tails, it's gray). If the coin comes down heads and you have the least inclination to make it two out of three tosses, you know it's the gray suit you want.
Emery Nemethy, Catawissa, Pennsylvania

17. THE CIVIL WAR RULE   Plan on using a man's weight in lead to kill one in battle.
Bob O'Halloran, radio talk-show host, Appleton, Wisconsin

18. FIRING A FOOTBALL   A quarterback has three seconds to fire the ball; after that he'll get sacked.
Bob O'Halloran, radio talk-show host, Appleton, Wisconsin

19. DESIGNING AN ELECTRIC MOTOR   The higher the frequency, the smaller the size of the motor. A motor designed to run on 400 Hz alternating current is about one-fourth the size of a motor designed for 60 Hz.   *Scott Parker, Beaumont, Texas*

20. COMMUNICATING IN A FOREIGN COUNTRY   In foreign countries, talk to people who speak a second language that you know too. Two people who both know even a little of the same language will communicate better than one who is fluent and one who is not.   *Peter Reimuller, Point Arena, California*

21. COMMUNICATING IN A FOREIGN COUNTRY   When traveling in a country whose language you don't know, the words for "yes," "no," "beer," "please," "thank you," "that," and as many numbers as possible will get you through about 90 percent of the situations you encounter. Memorizing complicated expressions is useless because you will not be able to understand the response. Grammar is irrelevant; correct pronunciation is vital. Act dumb, use your hands, and smile a lot.
Phil A. Schrodt, associate professor, Northwestern University

22. THE INJURY RULE OF SIX   It takes six weeks to completely recover from a musculoskeletal injury, though you begin to feel better in three weeks.   *Ned Frederick, writer, Exeter, New Hampshire*

23. WATERING YOUR PLANTS   For watering houseplants, when in doubt, don't. But for plants on your patio or windowsill, when in doubt, do.
Andrea Frankel, computer scientist, engineer, and holistic health practitioner, San Diego, California

24. STARTING A SHOW   The opening curtain of a play will rise seven to ten minutes after the announced time — later in bad weather. Movies, on the other hand, start precisely on time.
Kelly Yeaton, teacher and stage manager, State College, Pennsylvania

If you want to be friends with somebody else's dog, let the dog make the first move, and don't be too quick to respond.

Walter Pitkin, literary agent, Weston, Connecticut

25. USING A BIG WORD If you're writing something and you have to look up the definition of a word, you probably shouldn't use it. *Scott Parker, Beaumont, Texas*

26. FLYING AN ULTRALIGHT AIRCRAFT For the beginning ultralight-aircraft pilot, when the wind is good for kite flying, do that instead. *Tom Hammitt, Flying*

27. CHOOSING A LUXURY SHIP The longer and more expensive the cruise, the older the average age of the passengers. *Gerry M. Flick, M.D., ship's surgeon, S.S. Constitution*

28. EATING AT A VEGETARIAN RESTAURANT Don't order anything at a vegetarian restaurant that would have meat in it if served elsewhere. *Steve Carver, illustrator, Ithaca, New York*

29. APPRAISING ALLIGATORS The distance between an alligator's eyes, in inches, is its length, in feet. *Joan Isbell, horticulturist, Ithaca, New York*

30. GETTING USED TO COMPUTING It will take you about a year to feel comfortable using a home computer if you've never used one before. *Mark McMullen, accountant, Alexandria, Virginia*

31. COOLING YOUR CAR A car's air conditioner should produce air that is twenty-eight to thirty degrees below the outside temperature. *Scott Parker, Beaumont, Texas*

32. ENTERTAINING OLDER PEOPLE   Older people are consistently early arrivers. If you plan a luncheon for twelve-thirty, expect all the elderly guests to arrive by noon.
Berwyn Russell, retired, Indiana, Pennsylvania

33. HIDING FROM A TORNADO   A wet ditch is a good place to hide from a tornado as long as nearby electrical wires don't get the same idea.   *Mary Henshaw, Baytown, Texas*

34. AVOIDING LUNATICS   To avoid lunatics on city buses, sit in the middle of the bus. The friendly lunatics sit as close to the driver as they can, and the unfriendly ones sit as far away as they can.   *Keith Allan Hunter, computer operator, Denver, Colorado*

35. FALLING OUT OF SHAPE   It takes twice as long to fall out of shape as it took to get into shape.
Ned Frederick, writer, Exeter, New Hampshire

36. CHOOSING A WATERMELON   A watermelon is ripe when you hear *punk* rather than *pank* or *pink* when you tap it with your finger.   *Paul Kastner, Nagano, Japan*

37. WORKING WITH ROBOTS   You need one robotics technician for every four industrial robots.
Charles Stoehr, robotics technician, Cincinnati, Ohio

38. RIDING A MOTORCYCLE   New motorcyclists get cocky and reckless when they've put three thousand miles — or the equivalent of one trip across the United States — on their bikes.   *"Wolfman," Hell's Angel, Natchez, Mississippi*

39. LISTENING TO TENNIS   Your tennis shot will improve if you try to make it sound good.
Tom Robinson, computer programmer, Berkeley, California

40. PLANNING A CHEESE PLATE   When planning a cheese plate for a party, figure one-half ounce of cheese per guest.
Liz Biss, caterer, Ithaca, New York

41. BUYING CHEESE FOR A PARTY   For a wine and cheese party, count on having one pound of cheese for every five guests.
Maria Martin, art history student and former cheese shop employee, Kingston, Ontario

42. BUILDING AN IGLOO   An igloo should be built in an area where the snow is packed just loose enough to make a footprint, but not so loose that a footprint blows away in a high wind.
Dennis Eskow, science editor, Popular Mechanics

DEDE HATCH

43. MAKING SNOW Under optimum conditions, it takes about a foot of manmade snow to create the skiing conditions of three or more feet of natural snow.

Dennis Eskow, science editor, Popular Mechanics

44. LOOKING AT TRASH The average ten-ton pile of municipal trash contains six or seven tons of paper.

Scott Parker, Beaumont, Texas

45. WATCHING A DOG FIGHT   If two dogs are headed for a fight, and they appear about evenly matched, the dog on his home turf will win easily.   *Walter Pitkin, literary agent, Weston, Connecticut*

46. PREDICTING VOTER TURNOUT   You need a black population of 65 percent in an area to ensure that 50 percent of voters will be black. You lose 5 percentage points because of the lower median age of the black population, 5 percentage points for under-registration of blacks compared to whites, and 5 percentage points because blacks are less likely to vote than whites, even if they are registered.
Bill O'Hare, Joint Center for Political Studies, Washington, D.C.

47. TESTING A DIRECT-MAIL CAMPAIGN   For a reliable direct-mail test, you should mail enough pieces to get at least three hundred responses.   *Cathy Elton, circulation manager, Ithaca, New York*

48. THROWING A KNIFE   If your knife balances more than one inch from the tang on the handle side, it is handle heavy and should be thrown from the blade. Likewise, if it balances more than one inch from the tang on the blade side, it is blade heavy and should be thrown from the handle.
Survivalist, at a gun show in Lansing, New York

49. GRABBING GRADES   Grab as many good grades as possible early in the academic year. They'll come in handy as the year wears on.   *Dean Sheridan, Downey, California*

50. DRESSING FOR A SKI   When cross-country skiing, if you are warm when you first walk outside, you're wearing too much.   *Jeremy Bishop, cross-country ski instructor, Myers Point, New York*

51. LUNCHING WITH YOUR HELP   You have to have lunch with your cleaning lady once a month in order to keep her caring about your possessions.   *Laura H. Holmberg, attorney, Ithaca, New York*

52. MAKING HOT FUDGE   Your hot fudge is ready when you can write your name on the surface with a spoon without the letters disappearing before you finish writing.
Robin Masson, attorney and law professor, Ithaca, New York

53. WINNING A DUEL   When dueling with firearms, always aim lower than your opponent's vital area — to pierce the heart, aim at the knees.   *Jim Barber, historian, Springfield, Missouri*

54. CLIMBING NORTH IN THE SMOKIES   Climbing one thousand feet in altitude in the Great Smoky Mountains in North Carolina results in a change in vegetation analogous to traveling one hundred miles north — the Smoky Mountains at six thousand feet look like northern New England or southern Canada.
Doug Rugh, agricultural economist, Sevierville, Tennessee

Older people are consistently early arrivers. If you plan a luncheon for twelve-thirty, expect all the elderly guests to arrive by noon.

Berwyn Russell, retired, Indiana, Pennsylvania

JON REIS

55. THE OLYMPIC MOUNTAIN RULE   Because the underbrush grows so thick in the Olympic Mountains, hikers lost in this rainy region should seek high ground rather than follow water into low, impenetrable areas. From the high ground (most of which is no higher than six thousand feet) it's easy for a lost hiker to find the best route to safety.
William Krieger, English Department chairman, Gig Harbor, Washington

56. SAYING THINGS   If you find yourself thinking that something goes without saying, it is probably in the best interest of everyone involved to say it.
William Krieger, English Department chairman, Gig Harbor, Washington

57. SCREENING YOUR BABY FOR CYSTIC FIBROSIS
Kiss your baby. If he or she tastes extremely salty, check with your doctor about getting the baby tested for cystic fibrosis.
Tom Ferguson, M.D., editor, Medical Self-Care

58. POURING MILK FOR CEREAL   You have enough milk in the bowl when the edge of your pile of Cheerios first starts to move.   *Mike Rambo, photographer, Ithaca, New York*

59. PAINTING A CAR   When you're choosing paint for a car, navy blue, burgundy, and black cherry connote luxury. Bright yellow and red are considered sporty colors. Black and white are classics, while grays and silvers seem European. Greens are hard to sell.
Rich and Jean Taylor Constantine, quoting Debbie Weber, manager of color development design at Ford, in Parade

60. CHOOSING A CAR COLOR #1   One out of every ten new cars sold is white, the most popular color. It is also the safest color. The average pedestrian or motorist will spot a white car twelve times more quickly than a black one.
Rich and Jean Taylor Constantine, Parade

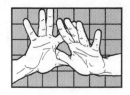

61. CHOOSING A CAR COLOR #2   When buying a new car, choose a color that matches the ads for your particular model. That's the color most likely to grab a used-car buyer's eye as well.   *Rich and Jean Taylor Constantine, Parade*

62. SELLING A NEW CAR   Your customer has decided to buy the car when he or she asks what colors are available. At that point, stop selling and close the deal.
Dirck Z. Meengs, management consultant, Canoga Park, California

63. WAITING IN LINE AT THE BANK   The number of minutes you will wait in a line at the bank is equal to the number of people ahead of you divided by the number of tellers times 2.75.
Chuck Davis, writer and broadcaster, Surrey, British Columbia

64. USING THE DRIVE-UP WINDOW   If there are more than three cars in line ahead of you at a bank or fast-food drive-up window, you'll save time if you get out of the car and go inside.
Bill Lowe, Birmingham, Alabama

65. WRITING A MAGAZINE ARTICLE   When writing a magazine article, begin with a snappy lead sentence, then write the piece to match the tone of the lead. Before submitting the article, delete the lead sentence.
Gordon Hard, assistant editor, Consumer Reports

66. PLANNING A COOPERATIVE HOUSEHOLD   Unless you are forming some sort of spiritual community, four is the best number of people for an adult cooperative household. It's manageable and provides a good level of intimacy. Any more and you will have a hotel or zoo situation.
Geanne Toma, massage therapist, Lebanon, New Hampshire

67. SWAPPING MUSCLE FOR FAT   About 40 percent of your body weight is muscle. If you swap nine pounds of muscle for nine pounds of fat, you'll shrink by about 1 percent because muscle is denser.   *Ned Frederick, writer, Exeter, New Hampshire*

68. COPPING A PLEA   If you get arrested, and you did it, and it's your first offense, skip the lawyer, plead guilty, and take your fine and/or probation. It will save you time and money, and it's the best "deal" most attorneys can arrange.
Carl Reddick, probation officer, Newport, Oregon

To find a lost golf ball, first look ten yards past where you think you hit it out, then look ten yards short, and finally look five yards farther into the rough.

Michael D. Miles, Aloha, Oregon

69. REACHING A GAS STATION If your tank is on empty and you're trying to make it to the next gas station, cut your speed to thirty-five miles per hour.
R. C. Woods, teacher, Miranda, California

70. CREATING A SNOW SCULPTURE A crew of three will spend two hours building for every foot of snow sculpture.
Mike McQueen, snow sculptor, Winter Park, Colorado

71. PASSING A CAR You can safely cut in front of the car you are passing when you can see its headlights in your inside rear-view mirror. *Leslie Simpson, Wollaston, Massachusetts*

72. NEGOTIATING A TRAFFIC CIRCLE When entering a traffic rotary, stay in the outside lane if you're taking the first exit, otherwise get in the inside lane.
Leslie Simpson, Wollaston, Massachusetts

73. ESTIMATING YOUR MAXIMUM OXYGEN UPTAKE
Your maximum oxygen uptake (VO_2 max.) is the best measure of your aerobic fitness. It is roughly equal to thirty times the miles you can run in twelve minutes. If you can run 1.6 miles in twelve minutes, your VO_2 max. is about $1.6 \times 30 = 48$ ml. O_2/kg./min. Elite athletes have values above 70 ml. O_2/kg./min. Average college-age men usually measure around 50, women about 20 percent less. A good minimum fitness standard is 40 ml./O_2/kg./min., regardless of age or sex. That works out to running a little over 1.3 miles in twelve minutes. *Ned Frederick, writer, Exeter, New Hampshire*

74. ANTICIPATING A PASTORATE As a general rule, a long pastorate is followed by a short one.
Fr. Emmet C. Smith, Largo, Florida

75. DEALING WITH DOUBT (SOCCER) When in doubt, kick it out. *Neil Hess, ski instructor, Syracuse, New York*

76. SELECTING A DOWNHILL SKI If you stand a ski vertically in front of you (don't wear heels), the top of the ski should curve directly over your head.
Neil Hess, ski instructor, Syracuse, New York

77. SELECTING A SKI POLE Turn the ski pole upside down, stand it next to you, and grasp the shaft directly below the basket. If your elbow makes a right angle, your pole is the right length.
Neil Hess, ski instructor, Syracuse, New York

78. RIDING A BUS On a Greyhound bus, the side with the bathroom has more legroom than the driver's side.
Neil Hess, ski instructor, Syracuse, New York

79. WORKING WITH SWEAT You lose about 2 to 3 percent of your body weight as sweat for every hour of heavy exercise, but don't confuse temporary dehydration for real weight loss. Losing more than 4 percent of your body weight as sweat can hurt your athletic performance. *Ned Frederick, writer, Exeter, New Hampshire*

80. MAINTAINING YOUR BODY FLUIDS You can maintain your fluid level by drinking at least four gulps of water every twenty minutes during prolonged exercise.
Ned Frederick, writer, Exeter, New Hampshire

81. BUYING A TYPEWRITER Portable typewriters cost four times more to operate than office models and last only one-fourth as long. *Scott Parker, Beaumont, Texas*

82. DEALING WITH DOGS Anything over forty-five minutes seems like forever to your dog. You will be greeted as enthusiastically coming back from a two-hour shopping trip as you will coming back from a two-day vacation.
Andrea Frankel, computer scientist, engineer, and holistic health practitioner, San Diego, California

83. ESTIMATING SIZE WITH MATCHES At arm's length, the width of a paper matchstick covers a space five yards wide one thousand yards away. The narrow width of a carpenter's pencil spans ten yards at that distance. Conversely, if you know the size of the object you're sighting, you can work backward to figure out how far away it is. *Bob Chaney, Carlsbad, California*

> The harder you have to brake to avoid hitting someone who pulls out in front of you, the sooner you'll have to brake for them to turn off.
>
> *Tania Werbizky, historic preservationist, Ithaca, New York*

84. LOADING A MUSKET   In a pinch, the proper powder charge for a muzzle-loading rifle or musket is the amount that will just cover the ball when you hold it in the hollow of your palm.
Bob Chaney, Carlsbad, California

85. ESTIMATING THE AGE OF A LOBSTER   Estimate the age of a large lobster by multiplying its weight, in pounds, by seven.   *Scott Parker, Beaumont, Texas*

86. JUDGING FIREWORKS   To judge the quality of a fireworks display, watch for color, especially blue. If you see good blues, you are watching a top-notch fireworks display.
Dr. John A. Conkling, executive director, American Pyrotechnics Association

87. AVOIDING A HELICOPTER   The dangerous gale-force rotor wash of a hovering helicopter extends outward to a distance three times the diameter of the main rotor.
David A. Shugarts, editor, Aviation Safety

88. THE VENTURE CAPITALIST RULE   Venture capitalists expect to get back five to ten times the amount of money they invested within three to five years.   *Scott Parker, Beaumont, Texas*

89. INVESTING VENTURE CAPITAL   Only one out of ten enterprises that a venture capitalist invests in will pay off — and it must pay for the losses on the other nine.
Walter Pitkin, literary agent, quoting Adam Smith, investment counselor

90. RUNNING AN AD AGENCY   In most ad agencies, one good writer can keep two good art directors busy.
Robert L. Bishopric, advertising executive, Miami, Florida

91. DRYING YOUR HANDS   If you are too busy to use hot-air hand dryers in public rest rooms, your lifestyle is too hectic for your own health.   *Gerald Gutlipp, mathematician, Chicago, Illinois*

92. DRIVING DEFENSIVELY   You should drive as if you are playing a video game with your last quarter. After ten minutes of this, you will have a better idea what defensive driving is all about.   *Gerald Gutlipp, mathematician, Chicago, Illinois*

93. TESTING YOUR COFFEE   If the cream swirls up brown, you have a cup of freshly brewed coffee. If it swirls up gray, the coffee has been sitting on the burner too long.
Rick Eckstrom, builder, Danby, New York

94. PLANNING YOUR TRAINING   Never increase your fitness training by more than 10 percent a week. An increase of 10 to 15 percent every three weeks makes more sense.
Ned Frederick, writer, Exeter, New Hampshire

95. THE RULES OF THREE   You should exercise at least three times a week. If you leave more than three days between exercise sessions, gains will be canceled out. Three weeks is about how long it takes your body to adjust to a new level of exercise.   *Ned Frederick, writer, Exeter, New Hampshire*

96. USING GRAPHITE TO SAVE WEIGHT   Replace an aluminum part with one made of graphite and you'll reduce its weight by at least 40 percent. If the weight reduction is less than 40 percent, there is something wrong with either your design or your calculations.
Thomas E. Keavney, aeronautical engineer, Norwalk, Connecticut

97. TESTING A WINE   Taste a young white wine that has been opened and kept in the refrigerator for a week. This will give you some idea of how an unopened bottle of the same wine will age in your wine cellar.   *Craig Goldwyn, publisher, International Wine Review*

98. FOLLOWING BACKFIRES   If a gasoline engine backfires through the carburetor, the fuel-air mixture is too lean. If it backfires through the tail pipe, the mixture is too rich.
Scott Parker, Beaumont, Texas

99. HIRING HELP FOR A PARTY   To make sure a formal dinner party runs smoothly, you will need one waiter per ten guests for a buffet supper or three waiters per twenty guests for seated dinner service. For receptions or cocktail parties, you will need one bartender, one kitchen helper (a waiter may double in this function), and one waiter per fifty guests. For more than fifty guests, you will need a supervisor as well.   *Food and Wine*

JON CRISPIN

100. HIRING A BARTENDER You need one bartender for
every one hundred guests at a party.
Joel Blumberg, student, Austin, Texas

101. CHOOSING A CHANDELIER The diagonal dimension of
a chandelier, in inches, should equal the diagonal dimension of
the dining room, in feet. Also, the diameter of the chandelier
should be at least twelve inches smaller than the diameter of the
dining room table. Otherwise, your dinner guests may hit their
heads when they stand up. *American Home Lighting Institute*

102. RECOVERING FROM LSD It takes ten years to recover
from serious use of LSD.
Leonard Cohen, poet and songwriter, quoted in USA Today

103. MAKING A FUSE IN A PINCH If your car blows a
weird-looking fuse and you don't have a spare, one wrap of cigarette pack foil around the old fuse will give you a twenty-amp
emergency fuse; two wraps will give you about thirty-five amps.
Douglass A. Pineo, biologist and falconer, Olympia, Washington

104. WAITING FOR A MAIL-ORDER RESPONSE The response to a direct-mail campaign peaks one week to ten days after you receive the first reply.
John Pitts, publicist, Boston, Massachusetts

105. BUDGETING A MAIL-ORDER BUSINESS In a mail-
order business, divide your budget into five equal parts: 20 percent for production costs, 20 percent for advertising, 20 percent
for overhead, 20 percent for profit, and 20 percent for hidden
costs. *Peter Reimuller, Point Arena, California*

106. CHARTING MAIL-ORDER RETURNS   If you're not getting 1 percent of your mail-order shipments returned, your product is underpriced.   *Peter Reimuller, Point Arena, California*

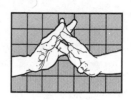

107. CUTTING YOUR HAIR   People who wear their hair short will generally need a haircut within a week after their hair looks perfect.   *Ann Kimbrough, Blaine, Tennessee*

108. TIMING YOUR GARAGE SALE   Hold a garage sale the first weekend of the month, because people who get paid monthly have more money to spend then.   *Ann Kimbrough, Blaine, Tennessee*

109. DRESSING YOURSELF   Wearing dark colors below the waist and light colors above is usually more visually appealing than the reverse.   *Donna Salyers, Cincinnati Enquirer*

110. MARKETING A FAD   You have ninety days to make and ship a novelty item and ninety days to sell it out. After that, inventory costs swallow up the profits.
Ellis E. Conklin, UPI feature writer, quoting Fred Reinstein, fad merchant

111. MOVING FOOD   Transportation costs are 60 percent of the price of food.   *Edward Martin, Davenport, Iowa*

112. POPPING CORN   You should get thirty-four cups of popcorn from a cup of kernels. Top-quality kernels will give you an extra ten cups.   *John O'Rourke, contributing editor, Let's Live*

113. POPPING CORN   Before making popcorn, check the temperature of the oil by placing three kernels in the pot as it heats; when all three pop, the oil is hot enough.
Richard L. Holloway, associate professor, University of Minnesota

114. LOOKING AT LETTERS   One out of every three business letters does nothing more than seek clarification of earlier correspondence.   *Scott Parker, Beaumont, Texas*

115. WRITING RULE   Writers overuse the word "massive." If you grunt and turn blue when you try to pick something up, it's massive. If you don't, it isn't.
Ben Hansen, editor, Beaumont (Texas) Enterprise

116. FOLLOWING CRIME   Bad weather is a cop's best friend. When it's raining and cold, nobody is outside committing crimes.
Eric Hanson, Houston Chronicle, quoting Houston Police Sergeant J. C. Mosier

DEDE HATCH

117. SCHEDULING CESAREANS If two elective Cesarean sections are scheduled on one morning, four Cesareans in all will be performed before the shift is over, and no one on the staff will get lunch.
Elizabeth Kasehagen, R.N., delivery room head nurse, Santa Barbara, California

118. PREDICTING RAIN If three pregnant women in a row check into the hospital with ruptured membranes but are not in labor, it will rain within twenty-four hours.
Elizabeth Kasehagen, R.N., delivery room head nurse, Santa Barbara, California

119. PAYING FOR AN AIRPLANE For all airplanes, from little ones to 747s, the price of the engine, or engines, is between 20 to 25 percent of the retail price of the airplane.
Richard L. Collins, editor in chief, Flying

120. AVOIDING LIGHTNING During an electrical storm, if the hair on your arms and head starts to stand on end, lightning is going to strike near you. Drop to your knees and bend forward, putting your hands on your knees. Don't place your hands on the ground or you will be vulnerable to ground current if a lightning bolt hits within fifty yards.
Scott Parker, Beaumont, Texas, quoting the National Fire Protection Association

121. MAKING A SPARK A spark needs 25,000 volts for every inch of air it has to jump.
Scott Parker, Beaumont, Texas, quoting Mr. Wizard

122. DRILLING FOR OIL Seven of every ten exploratory oil wells are dry holes. Of those that hit oil or gas, only one in forty is commercially successful. *Scott Parker, Beaumont, Texas*

123. FINDING DIAMONDS   Only one in five diamonds is of gem quality.   *Scott Parker, Beaumont, Texas*

124. CORRECTING YOUR INSTRUCTOR   When an instructor says, "Please correct me if I make a mistake," do it once and only once.   *Dean Sheridan, Downey, California*

125. FINDING YOUR COLLAPSE POINT   Your collapse point is about three times the average distance you swim, cycle, or run each day. For example, if you run an average of three miles a day, you should be able to run nine miles without stopping.
Ned Frederick, writer, Exeter, New Hampshire, quoting statistician Ken Young

126. PREPARING FOR A MARATHON   You need to run at least forty miles a week for at least six weeks to prepare for a marathon.   *L. M. Boyd, San Francisco Chronicle*

127. PREDICTING YOUR MARATHON TIME   You can predict your marathon time by multiplying your best ten-kilometer time by 4.65.
Ned Frederick, writer, Exeter, New Hampshire, quoting physiologist Jack Daniels

128. NOSING YOUR CAR TO A WALL   When you are parking a car head-on to a wall, turn on your high beams and look at the reflection on the wall as you slowly move closer. When the brightest part, the umbra, falls out of view, you are close enough.
Jon Roppolo, student, Flushing, New York

129. THE RADIO CONTEST RULE   The listener response to a radio call-in contest depends on the size of the prize. You can expect ten call-in contestants for every dollar you are giving away.
Don Burley, radio talk-show host, Kansas City, Kansas

130. STORING MUSICAL INSTRUMENTS   Changes in humidity over prolonged periods will affect the sound of wooden musical instruments. The higher the humidity, the duller and thicker a wooden instrument will sound.
Alan T. Whittemore, YMCA director, South Deerfield, Massachusetts

131. SHOWING OFF YOUR TARANTULAS   When stuffed tarantulas are displayed in a glass case, two out of four people will find them interesting. One person will refuse to look and one will want to inspect them closely. All will recoil at the idea of the glass top being removed.
Alan T. Whittemore, YMCA director, South Deerfield, Massachusetts

132. PLANNING POTATO SALAD   When making potato salad, figure 1½ medium potatoes and 1 egg per person.
Scott M. Kruse, biogeographer, Fresno, California

You will have more fun on your vacation if you maintain a mental age of eighteen or less. Act just old enough to make your travel connections and stay out of trouble.
Joe Schwartz, editor, Danby, New York

133. RESTORING OLD MOTORCYCLES Somebody who says more than two or three sentences about his current motorcycle restoration project is never going to finish it. In a year, make him a decent offer for the half-assembled wreck.
Jake Williams, Aberdeenshire, Scotland

134. KEEPING YOURSELF IN STRINGS The first string that breaks on a guitar is usually the high E (the first string); next likely to break are the G and D strings (the third and fourth).
Ellen Klaver, musician, Boulder, Colorado

135. CHOOSING A MOVIE #1 If you've heard of the stars of a movie but you haven't heard about the movie itself, it's probably a stinker.
Bruce Reznick, associate professor of mathematics, Urbana, Illinois

136. CHOOSING A MOVIE #2 If a new movie is on TV or cable and you haven't heard of it, it's probably a stinker.
Bruce Reznick, associate professor of mathematics, Urbana, Illinois

137. CHOOSING A MOVIE #3 A movie released to the public before it's reviewed is a stinker.   *Dean Sheridan, Downey, California*

138. WATCHING YOUR STEP The feller that agrees with everything you say is a fool or he is getting ready to skin you.
Kin Hubbard, Brown County, Indiana, c. 1920, via Phil A. Schrodt

139. SUFFERING CULTURE SHOCK Culture shock occurs only in the first three foreign countries you visit. After that, you subconsciously focus on similarities rather than differences.
Gary Gaile, geographer

140. AVOIDING A BUSY AIRPORT Thursday is the busiest day of the week at U.S. airports. *Scott Parker, Beaumont, Texas*

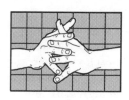

141. EXPLAINING A MATHEMATICAL THEOREM If you can't explain a mathematical theorem to a ten-year-old, you don't understand it yourself.
G. S. Tahim, mathematician, Bloomington, Indiana

142. INVESTING YOUR MONEY The highest rate of return per invested dollar of capital is in the broadcasting business. The oil business finishes two places behind worm farming.
Scott Parker, Beaumont, Texas, quoting Royalty Owners Action Report

143. TIMING A GIG If your musical engagement is less than two hours long, you will spend as much time setting up and taking down equipment as you will playing music.
Ellen Klaver, musician, Boulder, Colorado

144. WRITING A COMPUTER PROGRAM #1 When writing a long computer program, figure out the data storage first, the input and output next, and only then write the parts of the program that actually do the work.
Phil A. Schrodt, associate professor, Northwestern University

145. WRITING A COMPUTER PROGRAM #2 Write the documentation for a program before you write the program itself. In other words, figure out how you are going to explain the program to the user, then write the program to fit the explanation.
Phil A. Schrodt, associate professor, Northwestern University,

146. WRITING A COMPUTER PROGRAM #3 To write a good program, write and debug the entire program, get it documented and working perfectly, then start over again from scratch based on what you learned the first time through. This process can be repeated as many as four times and still be cost-effective, but you should always do it at least once.
Phil A. Schrodt, associate professor, Northwestern University

147. WRITING A COMPUTER PROGRAM #4 In most computer programs, 10 percent of the program accounts for 90 percent of the processing time. Finding and rewriting this part of the program so that it runs fast is always cost-effective.
Phil A. Schrodt, associate professor, Northwestern University

148. WRITING A COMPUTER PROGRAM #5 No good computer program can be written by more than ten people. The best programs are written by one or two people.
Phil A. Schrodt, associate professor, Northwestern University

If you're traveling a long distance by car and you need to tell someone when you expect to arrive, divide the distance by fifty to obtain the number of hours your drive will take. This usually will allow for a leisurely drive without causing undue anxiety for those awaiting your arrival.

Robert Hastings, master chief petty officer, U.S. Coast Guard

149. THE BURGLARY RULE OF THREE   To determine the true value of items stolen in a burglary, take the reported value and divide by three.
Thomas O. Marsh, writer and former police chief, Fairfield, Ohio

150. LOOKING AT EYELASHES   The youngest child has the longest eyelashes.   *Sarah Bynum, Brookline, Massachusetts*

151. MAKING TOFU One pound of soybeans yields 2½ pounds of tofu. *Robert A. Shapiro, charter pilot, Ithaca, New York*

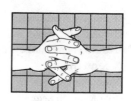

152. PLAYING ROCK AND ROLL IN NEW YORK CITY
When your rock and roll band can play forty-five minutes of original music, it is ready to look for work in New York City bars.
Kid with Mohawk haircut and engineer's boots, Ithaca, New York

153. FALLING ASLEEP TO MUSIC If you want to fall asleep with the stereo on, turn the volume down to a level that is too quiet for when you are awake. In less than five minutes, that level will feel comfortable, but if you're still awake in fifteen minutes, you may have to turn the volume down again.
Rusty Cartmill, student newspaper editor, University of Georgia

154. SWIMMING, RUNNING, AND CYCLING Swimming one mile is equivalent to running five miles or cycling twelve miles.
Ned Frederick, writer, Exeter, New Hampshire

155. GETTING A MORTGAGE When interest rates are high, banks will allow you to spend up to 33 percent of your total income on the principal, interest, and insurance on a home mortgage. When interest rates are low, the limit decreases to 25 percent of your total income. *Scott Parker, Beaumont, Texas*

156. CHECKING YOUR CHARCOAL Your fire is ready when the charcoal is light gray. Test the heat by holding your hand, palm side down, over the coals at grid level and counting the seconds you can hold it there. Five seconds indicates a low temperature fire; four seconds, medium temperature; three seconds, medium-high; two seconds, hot; one second indicates that the fire is too hot. *Carolyn Flournoy, Gannett News Service*

157. WATCHING TELLERS The average bank teller loses about $240 a year.
Scott Parker, Beaumont, Texas, quoting the Wall Street Journal

158. RUNNING AND TALKING While exercising, if you can't maintain a conversation without gasping for breath, you are probably working beyond your aerobic target zone.
Kurt Ulrich, exercise specialist, Tompkins County Hospital, Ithaca, New York

159. WAITING FOR THE MARKET TO PLUNGE A stock market low occurs every four years. *Scott Parker, Beaumont, Texas*

160. WATCHING A WINERY A winery's standards start to slip if it produces more than fifty thousand cases of wine per year.
Richard Graff, chairman and chief operating officer, Chalone, Inc., Sonoma County, California

> In house building, the lighter the framing, the more recent the construction.
>
> *Greg Koos, McLean County Historical Society, Bloomington, Illinois*

JON REIS

161. SWITCHING YOUR BRAND One out of ten cigarette smokers switches brands every year.
L. M. Boyd, *San Francisco Chronicle*

162. LEARNING A LANGUAGE About 150 to 200 hours of instruction and $1,500 worth of tapes and classes should result in creditable speaking ability in French, Spanish, or German. For Oriental and Middle Eastern languages, figure two or three times longer. *Boardroom Reports*

163. APPRECIATING CLASSICAL MUSIC If a piece of classical music was written after you were born, you are not obliged to appreciate it. *Francis Cooke, composer (born 1910)*

164. THE WEEKEND SAILOR'S RULE The distance traveled in three minutes, measured in yards, divided by one hundred, equals your speed in knots. Conversely, your speed in knots, times one hundred, is how many yards you will travel in three minutes. Here's an example: Fifteen knots equals fifteen hundred yards every three minutes.
Robert Hastings, master chief petty officer, U.S. Coast Guard

165. THE DRIVING RULE OF FIFTY If you're traveling a long distance by car and you need to tell someone when you expect to arrive, divide the distance by fifty to obtain the number of hours your drive will take. This usually will allow for a leisurely drive without causing undue anxiety for those awaiting your arrival. *Robert Hastings, master chief petty officer, U.S. Coast Guard*

166. SELECTING A RIPE HONEYDEW MELON   A honeydew melon is ripe if the end opposite the stem gives easily when you press it with your thumb. Also, when you rub the skin with your finger, it should feel slightly sticky.
Cindy Watanabe, Honolulu, Hawaii

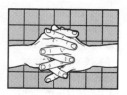

167. BUYING AN EGGPLANT   To avoid a seedy eggplant, choose one that has a round scar at the end opposite the stem. An oval scar means a female plant, which will have more seeds.
Cindy Watanabe, Honolulu, Hawaii

168. DOUBLING A BABY   The average newborn will double its weight in six months.   *L. M. Boyd, San Francisco Chronicle*

169. WRITING IN ENGLISH   About half the elements used in writing are chosen by the writer; the rest are required by the structure of the language.   *Scott Parker, Beaumont, Texas*

170. SELLING CONDOMINIUMS #1   Two out of three people who buy lower-priced condominiums really want to buy a house instead.   *Vince Mooney, real estate broker, Tulsa, Oklahoma*

171. SELLING CONDOMINIUMS #2   To sell, condominiums should be priced at least 25 percent lower than the starting price of houses in the area. For best success, they should be priced 50 percent below nearby houses. People who buy a $50,000 condo want to live in a $100,000 neighborhood.
Vince Mooney, real estate broker, Tulsa, Oklahoma

172. SELLING CONDOMINIUMS #3   Any customer who comes to a condominium sales office and asks to see all the models (one-, two-, and three- bedroom units) will never buy anything.   *Vince Mooney, real estate broker, Tulsa, Oklahoma*

173. CHOOSING A CHRISTMAS TREE   When you're choosing a Christmas tree, rotate the tip of a branch between your forefinger and thumb. If the tree is fresh, you won't end up with a handful of needles.   *David and Penny Russell, Dilltown, Pennsylvania*

174. KEEPING A CHRISTMAS TREE   A fresh Christmas tree should last four weeks without shedding its needles.
American Christmas Tree Association

175. PERUSING A STOCK OFFERING #1   For a young company going public that hasn't produced much in the way of earnings, look at the ratio of its total offering price to its annual sales. A healthy market-capitalization-to-sales ratio should exceed 2.7.
Francine Schwadel, staff reporter, quoting various experts in the Wall Street Journal

Hold a nickel next to the tip of your pool cue. The tip of the cue is the right shape if its silhouette matches the curve of the nickel's edge.

Michael Rider, art director, Ithaca, New York

176. PERUSING A STOCK OFFERING #2 Established companies generally go public for $10 a share or more. An offering price of less than $1 a share signals an extraordinary amount of risk, while a price of $1 to $5 a share means the issue is very speculative.
Francine Schwadel, staff reporter, quoting various experts in the Wall Street Journal

177. CHOOSING THE RIGHT CAMEL Don't choose a camel that trembles while sitting. This means its front legs are bad.
Lauren Stockbower, photojournalist, in Empire/Pan Am Clipper magazine

178. TRAVELING BY CAMEL A good camel should be able to travel eighty to one hundred kilometers per day easily.
Lauren Stockbower, photojournalist, in Empire/Pan Am Clipper magazine

179. CHECKING A PEARL To tell if a pearl is genuine, rub it against your teeth. A fake pearl will feel smooth; the real thing will grate. *Quinith Janssen, pearl expert, USAir magazine*

180. FINDING AN ATHLETE'S IDEAL WEIGHT An endurance athlete's ideal weight, in pounds, is twice his height, in inches. *Ned Frederick, writer, Exeter, New Hampshire*

181. RACING A BOBSLED In bobsled competition, every second lost at the start costs three seconds at the finish. On a luge run, the time lost at the start is multiplied by four at the finish.
ABC-TV commentator, 1984 Winter Olympics

182. ADDING CANNED LAUGHTER   A TV sitcom needs at least a slight chuckle from the audience every thirty seconds. Otherwise, you have to add a laugh track.
Rick Mitz, author of The Great TV Sitcom Book

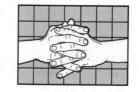

183. ADDRESSING THE CLERGY #1   Never call any cleric, male or female, "Reverend" — it's bad English.
Rev. Halsey DeW. Howe, Saint Mark's Church, Springfield, Vermont

184. ADDRESSING THE CLERGY #2   Always call a Roman Catholic priest "Father" unless he is wearing some purple. Then call him "Bishop" or "Your Excellency."
Rev. Halsey DeW. Howe, Saint Mark's Church, Springfield, Vermont

185. ADDRESSING THE CLERGY #3   When in doubt, call a Protestant minister or a rabbi "Doctor." Even if the person isn't a doctor, he or she will be flattered.
Rev. Halsey DeW. Howe, Saint Mark's Church, Springfield, Vermont

186. ADDRESSING THE CLERGY #4   Always call a male Episcopal priest "Father." If he doesn't like it, he will tell you. If he does like it, he will beam all over!
Rev. Halsey DeW. Howe, Saint Mark's Church, Springfield, Vermont

187. ADDRESSING THE CLERGY #5   If you don't know what to call a woman Episcopal priest, cheer up — no one else does!   *Rev. Halsey DeW. Howe, Saint Mark's Church, Springfield, Vermont*

188. VENTILATING YOUR ATTIC   You need 1 square foot of attic vent for every 150 square feet of attic ceiling area.
Rick Eckstrom, builder, Danby, New York

189. AVERAGING THE WEATHER   The average of the average temperatures across North America is usually fairly even. When it's cold in the West, it's warm in the East, and vice versa.
Walter Pitkin, literary agent, Weston, Connecticut

190. WRITING A RÉSUMÉ   The longer your job title and job description, the less important you are.
Dean Sheridan, Downey, California

191. PROFITING FROM ADVERTISING   For a going company, the increase in profits caused by advertising is usually equal to the amount spent on advertising.
Peter Reimuller, Point Arena, California

192. LISTENING TO JIGS AND REELS   The way to tell the difference between a jig and a reel is to sing along with it. With a jig, you will be able to sing "jiggity jig, jiggity jig." If the tune is a reel, you can sing, "I think I can, I think I can."   *Wild Asparagus band*

To solve a crime, remember two things: The most obvious solution is probably the correct one, and, if you've eliminated all the other possibilities, whatever is left, however improbable, is what happened.

Stephen G. Michaud, quoting FBI Agent Howard D. Teten, quoting Sherlock Holmes in the New York Times

193. MEETING PEOPLE AT PARTIES At a party or public event, the person who laughs spontaneously at the same time you do probably is worth cultivating as a friend.
Kelly Yeaton, teacher and stage manager, State College, Pennsylvania

194. ARRANGING A DATE The first thing to get when arranging a date is the other person's phone number, in case you want to call it off. *Janet Berrest, secretary and writer, Philadelphia, Pennsylvania*

195. CATCHING A COLD You will catch a cold within two weeks of starting a new job.
Beth Blinick, sales promotion and marketing, Skokie, Illinois

196. PICKING A WINNER AT THE TRACK #1 When you're at the harness track, bet on a horse that runs a fast first half mile and has final quarter times under thirty-one seconds.
Don Valliere, track manager and author, Fort Erie, Ontario

197. PICKING A WINNER AT THE TRACK #2 It's usually safe to bet on a horse that has just been assigned a leading full-time driver. The trainer probably believes the horse is ready to win. *Don Valliere, track manager and author, Fort Erie, Ontario*

198. PROLONGING LIFE Ninety percent of the patients who come into an internist's office will get well no matter what the doctor does. Two percent will die despite everything the doctor does for them. It is the other 8 percent that the internist, with the support of the rest of the medical profession, can help the most.
Walter Pitkin, literary agent, quoting a Connecticut internist

199. THE DINING-OUT RULE The complete meal will cost about two times the price of the entrées.
Richard Patching, acoustician, Calgary, Alberta

200. THE RULE OF RHUBARB Three pounds of rhubarb makes two pies or one imperial gallon of homemade wine.
Richard Patching, acoustician, Calgary, Alberta

201. BUYING GROCERIES Shopping for groceries while hungry will triple the cost of the trip.
Lexy B. Rockhold, housewife, Drumright, Oklahoma

202. KEEPING BEES A skilled beekeeper can get as much as one hundred pounds of honey per hive per year.
Dave Peyton, Gannett News Service

203. INSURING A HELICOPTER Insurance underwriters used to have a rule for approving helicopter pilots for commercial operations: Pick a pilot with at least one thousand hours of rotary-wing experience. If a pilot has survived that long, he has probably encountered every hazard, from tail rotor and engine failures to tail strikes and ground resonance vibrations.
AOPA Pilot

204. WORRYING ABOUT THE BOMB When the movies stop mentioning the bomb, you know it's on everybody's mind.
Tom Shales, movie critic, National Public Radio

205. FEELING YOUR OIL Rub a little of your motor oil between your thumb and forefinger. If you can feel any grit, it's time to change your oil. *Donny Bates, gas station attendant, Cincinnati, Ohio*

206. CHIPPING THE BALL In golf, to make your chipping iron shots rise, hit down on the ball.
Tom Robinson, computer programmer, Berkeley, California

207. DEALING WITH CUSTOMERS Customers are most difficult to deal with during the full moon. The next most trying phase is the new moon.
Georgia Chapman, pharmacist, Bedford, Virginia

208. EATING IN CAFETERIAS Cafeterias serve institution-grade foods. Never imagine anything else.
Dean Sheridan, Downey, California

209. WORKING ON A PROJECT When working on a project that requires both humans and inanimate objects, always remember: Bricks are more reliable than people.
Joseph Nunziata III, accountant and actor, Bellerose, New York

If you buy a newspaper, read it as soon as you can, and in one sitting if possible. If you postpone reading the paper or interrupt yourself halfway through, you probably won't get back to it.

D. Branner, New York City

210. BORROWING THINGS   Never loan a possession unless you borrow an item of equal importance at the same time.
Steven Kropper, Ithaca, New York

211. LEAVING A TIP   Tip the waiter 20 percent of the bill minus 2 percent for each instance of poor service minus 5 percent for anything spilled on you.   *Paul Egert, South Plainfield, New Jersey*

212. MAINTAINING A USED AIRPLANE During the first five years of ownership, the cost of maintenance will nearly equal the purchase price of a used airplane.
Sarah Padula, teacher and pilot, Freeville, New York

213. THE LIBRARY RULE OF 20/80 Twenty percent of a library's patrons account for 80 percent of the library's use. Twenty percent of the books in a library account for 80 percent of the library's use. *Scott Parker, Beaumont, Texas*

214. HEATING A RENTAL UNIT You can expect a 40 percent reduction in energy consumption when a tenant assumes responsibility for the energy bills. *Larry Beck, joiner, Lansing, New York*

215. USING WORDS The average American has a vocabulary of about three thousand words. *Scott Parker, Beaumont, Texas*

216. DEALING WITH A NEW AGE EVANGELIST If a person has experienced only one kind of transformational experience, take everything he or she says with a lot of salt.
Andrea Frankel, computer scientist, engineer, and holistic health practitioner, San Diego, California

217. TESTING A BONE FOR FOSSILIZATION It's only a fossil if it's heavy and solid. *Scott Parker, Beaumont, Texas*

218. GETTING SOME SLEEP Each hour of sleep before midnight is equal to two hours of sleep after midnight.
Nick O'Conner, San Francisco, California

219. CALCULATING NUTRIENT DENSITY To calculate a product's nutrient density (the ratio of nutrients to calories): (1) Add the percentage of U.S. Recommended Daily Allowances per serving for the first eight nutrients listed on the label. (2) Divide this total by the number of calories per serving. (3) Multiply by one hundred to obtain a percentage. The minimum score for good nutritional value is thirty-two, but higher is better.
Modern Maturity

220. DROPPING A GLASS If a cafeteria glass bounces more than once, it will break. *Sharon K. Yntema, writer, Ithaca, New York*

221. FEEDING A PIKE Given a choice, northern pike prefer prey that is about a third of their own length.
Phil Johnson, State University of New York, Albany, in The New York State Conservationist

> If you are north of the equator, don't buy property on the south side of a jetty. The drift of the ocean is from south to north, and the beach will erode south of any protrusion that blocks the drift.
>
> *Carol Terrizzi, artist and graphic designer, Ithaca, New York*

JON CRISPIN

222. WEIGHING A PIKE You can estimate the weight, in pounds, of a northern pike by cubing its length, in inches, and dividing by 3,500.
Phil Johnson, State University of New York, Albany, in The New York State Conservationist

223. ESTIMATING THE WEIGHT OF A TROUT You can estimate the weight of a brown trout if you remember that a twenty-inch fish weighs three pounds and a twenty-five-inch fish weighs five pounds. For every inch over twenty-five inches, add one pound to the weight of the fish. For example, a twenty-seven-inch brown trout weighs seven pounds.
Thomas Lack, somewhere on the east shore of Lake Michigan

224. LEVELING A TRAILER When using screw-type jacks for leveling a trailer, install the front jacks, crank them up, and level the trailer. Drop down one turn, put the rear jacks under the back, then crank the rear up two turns. Crank down one turn in front and the jacks should all be snug and the trailer level.
Scott M. Kruse, biogeographer, Fresno, California

225. TAPING WIRES It takes four layers of electrical tape to waterproof an electrical connection properly.
Dennis Pollack, builder, Danby, New York

226. HITCHHIKING IN MISSISSIPPI In Mississippi, a man hitchhiking alone will be passed by about two hundred cars before one will stop. Having a woman companion or wearing a military uniform will cut the wait by more than half; being accompanied by another man or a dog will double or triple it.
Pierce Butler, Natchez, Mississippi

227. ADJUSTING AN EXERCISE MACHINE When you work out with an exercise machine, choose a weight setting that lets you do eight to twelve repetitions comfortably. If you must struggle to get beyond five, the setting is too heavy. If you complete ten without feeling any fatigue at all, it is too light.
Bottom Line/Personal

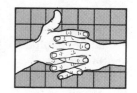

228. MAINTAINING FIGHTER AIRCRAFT Northrop Corporation estimates that a unit of twenty-four F-20s can be kept flying by 164 people; a unit of F-16s requires 323 people; and a unit of F-15s, 476. *Gregg Easterbrook, staff writer, The Atlantic Monthly*

229. INTERPRETING HANDWRITING A woman who makes large, long loops in her y's and g's is highly affectionate and responsive. *L. M. Boyd, San Francisco Chronicle*

230. LOOKING AT HANDWRITING Handwriting that contains a haphazard mix of capital and lowercase letters was most likely written by a man.
Sarah Padula, teacher and pilot, Freeville, New York

231. WORKING WITH PRESSURE Ten feet of elevation gives four pounds of pressure in a water pipe.
Peter Reimuller, Point Arena, California

232. THE OFT-SUBMITTED RULE OF TWICE Twice around the thumb is once around the wrist. Twice around the wrist is once around the neck. Twice around the neck is once around the waist. *D. Dropsho, Madison, Wisconsin.*

233. CLIMBING ABOARD A BOAT If there are three or more inches of water in the bilge of a rowboat, don't get in it. Your weight will be enough to capsize the boat.
Andrew Kuchinsky, boater, Boston, Massachusetts

234. THE RIDGWAY WIND-CHILL FACTOR To estimate the wind-chill factor, subtract the wind velocity from the temperature. *Becky Ridgway, Wichita, Kansas*

235. WRITING A SPEECH Professional speech writers budget an hour and a half of research, thinking, and writing for every minute of a speech. *Canadian Business*

236. PREPARING A SPEECH A good five-minute speech requires one month's advance notice. A fifteen-minute speech requires a week's notice. A one-hour speech requires no advance notice. *Dirck Z. Meengs, management consultant, Canoga Park, California*

Handwriting that contains a haphazard mix of capital and lower case letters was most likely written by a man.

Sarah Padula, teacher and pilot, Freeville, New York

237. KEEPING UP WITH NEWSPAPERS If you buy a newspaper, read it as soon as you can, and in one sitting if possible. If you postpone reading the paper or interrupt yourself halfway through, you probably won't get back to it.
D. Branner, New York City

238. DEALING WITH LARGE SUMS OF MONEY Large sums of money engender both stinginess and personal extravagance. *D. Branner, New York City*

239. WRITING Limit yourself to one thought per sentence. The sentences will end up being different lengths because some thoughts will be long and some short. The result will be a conversational tone.
Albert Joseph, president, International Writing Institute, Inc., in Industry Week

240. RESTING AFTER EXERCISE Allow twenty-four hours of recovery for every hour of highly stressful workout.
Ned Frederick, writer, Exeter, New Hampshire

241. SOLVING A CRIME To solve a crime, remember two things: The most obvious solution is probably the correct one; and, if you've eliminated all the other possibilities, whatever is left, however improbable, is what happened.
Stephen G. Michaud, quoting FBI Agent Howard D. Teten, quoting Sherlock Holmes, in the New York Times

242. CHASING RATS IN NEW YORK CITY There is one rat for every New Yorker — or one New Yorker for every rat.
Lee Jones, spokesman for Mayor Edward I. Koch, in the Cincinnati Enquirer

243. USING A MICROWAVE If you are not sure if a piece of glassware is safe for use in a microwave oven, pour one-half cup of water into a separate glass measure. Place both the measure and the dish you are testing inside your oven and run it at full power for one minute. Check the temperature of the dish and of the water. If the water is warm but the dish is cool, it's safe for microwave cooking. *Better Homes and Gardens*

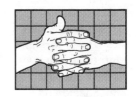

244. LOWERING YOUR TRAVEL RISKS Pick a hotel room between the third and sixth floors. Three floors puts you above street attacks and random shootings, while six floors will keep you in range of a cherry picker or fireman's ladder if the place goes up in flames.
Stephen Kindel, quoting Eugene Mastrangelo and Jerry Hoffman, security analysts, in Savvy

245. GROUPING YOUR BULLETS A gun shooting at its best usually produces round, uniform bullet patterns on a target. If your bullet groups are generally uniform but with an occasional random flyer, the problem is probably the ammo. But if the flyers tend to go in the same direction, the problem is more likely caused by the rifle. *Jim Carmichael, Shooting Times*

246. TRYING TO GET PREGNANT It's time to consult a fertility specialist if you haven't gotten pregnant after twelve months of trying.
Dr. June Reinisch, syndicated columnist, United Feature Syndicate

247. THE HOTEL RULE OF THREE The third owner of a hotel will make a profit. By that time, the cost of the building will reflect its true market value.
Dirck Z. Meengs, management consultant, Canoga Park, California

248. INSTALLING A FAN IN A SUN ROOM To move hot air out of an overheated sun room, you need a thermostatically controlled fan with a flow rate of four to six cubic feet per minute per square foot of glass in the sun room.
Jan F. Kreider, consulting engineer, Popular Science

249. FOLLOWING ANOTHER CAR Leave a three-second interval between you and the car in front of you. This provides enough room to stop at any speed.
Dirck Z. Meengs, management consultant, Canoga Park, California

250. FOLLOWING ANOTHER CAR Regardless of your speed, in good weather you should stay at least two full seconds behind the car ahead. When the weather is bad, increase the time to three seconds or more. *Chris Carter, East Lansing, Michigan*

JON REIS

251. SPEEDING UP AN AIRPLANE   If you put a larger engine in your airplane, you can expect the cruise speed to increase by one-third the percentage you've increased the power. For example, pump up the power by 30 percent and you'll see a 10 percent increase in your cruise speed.   *Bill Cox, Plane and Pilot*

252. THE QUICK RULE OF CONVERSION   To quickly convert degrees Celsius to Fahrenheit, double the temperature and add thirty. Thus, 10° C is 50° F, and 20° C is 70° F. To convert from degrees Fahrenheit to Celsius, subtract thirty and divide by two. The exact formula is $F = \frac{9}{5}C + 32$.
Stephen J. Lambrechts-Forester, Green Oaks, Illinois

253. THE ALBUM RULE OF SINGLES   On a pop or rock music album, the first and second songs on side A, the first song on side B, and the title track (if there is one and it doesn't fit into any of the other three categories) will be released as singles.
Chris Carter, East Lansing, Michigan

254. CALLING A COLLEGE DORM   Most dormitory phones are answered just after the second ring. If a call hasn't been answered by the fourth ring, chances are it won't be.
Chris Carter, East Lansing, Michigan

255. MAKING PANCAKES   Judge your pancakes by the third one you cook; the first two are worse than the rest of the batch.
Mark McMullen, accountant, Alexandria, Virginia

256. BUILDING STAIRS   Any combination of riser height plus tread width that adds up to 17½ inches will be comfortable to use and will not cause people to stumble.   *Don Naish, Dryden, Michigan*

257. MAKING A PLEASING RECTANGLE The closer the proportions of a rectangle are to three by five, the more pleasing it is to the eye. *Don Naish, Dryden, Michigan*

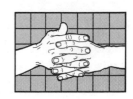

258. BUYING COMPUTER EQUIPMENT When buying a computer system, particularly a computer graphics system, figure that for every dollar you spend, you'll end up with fifty cents' worth of equipment.
Kim Davis, software developer, Davis Graphic Services, Lansing, New York

259. SORTING OUT INTERSTATES #1 Odd-numbered interstate highways go north and south. Even-numbered interstates go east and west. Interstate numbers increase from west to east, and from south to north, as do many U.S. and state highways.
Bob Horton, consultant and writer, St. Petersburg, Florida

260. SORTING OUT INTERSTATES #2 Three-digit interstate highways typically go around cities when the first digit is even and go through cities when the first digit is odd.
Bob Horton, consultant and writer, St. Petersburg, Florida

261. DRIVING ON INTERSTATES When you're driving on an interstate with three or more lanes per side, stay as close to the middle lane as possible. That way you can avoid the hassle of having your lane end or having it "peel off" to either the right or the left. This is a particularly good rule to remember in heavy traffic. *Bob Horton, consultant and writer, St. Petersburg, Florida*

262. PRODUCING CHAMPAGNE To be properly stocked, a winery should have in its cellars an amount of champagne equal to the amount it can sell in three years.
Barry Bassin, wine merchant, New York City

263. TASTING A CHAMPAGNE You should not have to swallow a mouthful of good champagne twice in order to taste the wine around the bubbles. Once should be enough.
Barry Bassin, wine merchant, New York City

264. GROWING FINGERNAILS The longer your fingers, the faster your nails grow. *Scott Parker, Beaumont, Texas*

265. CATCHING A LIAR A good liar will look his victim in the eyes in an attempt to be convincing. Two tip-offs are an increase in his rate of blinking and overly complicated explanations. *Dr. Joyce Brothers, Syracuse Post Standard*

266. STARING AT SOMEONE Two people who stare each other in the eye for sixty seconds straight will soon either be fighting or making love. *Pierce Butler, Natchez, Mississippi*

267. PLANNING SPACE FOR A BUSINESS MEETING For a business meeting, find a room large enough to provide at least thirty square feet of space per person.
Cally Arthur, managing editor, Alpine, New York

268. AVOIDING DANGEROUS TOYS If a toy is smaller than a child's fist, don't buy it; if it can fit in the mouth, it can also get caught in the throat.
Elaine Tyrrell, Children's and Recreational Products Program, Consumer Product Safety Commission

269. SAVING ON COOLING For every one degree you raise the temperature setting on your air conditioner thermostat, you increase energy efficiency by 3 percent.
"Morning Edition," National Public Radio

270. FINDING MONEY FOR COLLEGE Add 5 percent of the value of your assets to your adjusted gross income and divide this figure by the annual costs of the college you are considering. If this yields a result of six or less, you will probably qualify for some sort of loan or financial assistance.
Robert Leider, author of Don't Miss Out

271. SHOOTING AT DUCKS For every 1,000 ducks shot at with lead shot, 155 will be bagged and 46 wounded. For every 1,000 shot at with steel shot, 114 will be bagged and 51 wounded. At ranges greater than thirty-five yards, lead shot cripples more ducks than steel shot.
Jack Mosher, wildlife biologist, South Berne, New York, in The New York State Conservationist

272. THE IRONY OF DENTS RULE   If you don't get a dent in your new car in the first week, you probably won't get one in the first year.   *Lory Peck, social worker, Albany, New York*

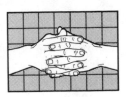

273. RON'S TAX RULE #1   If in doubt, deduct it.
Ronald R. Hodge, investment executive and commercial pilot, Long Beach, California

274. RON'S TAX RULE #2   If you aren't notified that you'll be audited by the IRS, you probably forgot to deduct something. If you aren't called in for an audit within a year of filing your return, chances are that you won't be audited for that year.
Ronald R. Hodge, investment executive and commercial pilot, Long Beach, California

275. ANSWERING AN ESSAY QUESTION   Answer an essay question as if you were talking to your parents.
Dean Sheridan, Downey, California

276. SAVING YOUR HAY AND YOUR WOOD   On the first of February you should still have half your hay and half your firewood.   *Susan Waterstripe, town supervisor, Sheds, New York*

277. CUTTING FIREWOOD #1   It takes twenty-four manhours for a nonprofessional logger to bring a cord of wood from the stump to the stove.
Michael Blyskal, state real estate appraiser, Albany, New York, in The New York State Conservationist

278. CUTTING FIREWOOD #2   It takes ten eight-inch maple trees to make a cord of wood.
Michael Blyskal, state real estate appraiser, Albany, New York, in The New York State Conservationist

279. PRODUCING SILK   It takes 110 silkworm cocoons to make a tie; 630 to make a blouse. A heavy silk kimono might equal the work of 3,000 silkworms, and they will have eaten 135 pounds of mulberry leaves.   *Nina Hyde, writer, National Geographic*

280. CHECKING CANNED FOOD   When you open a can or bottle, keep a thumb on the top. If the top pops up when you break the seal, it's fine; if it pops down, throw it out.
Leslie Simpson, Wollaston, Massachusetts

281. MAKING A SALE   A manufacturer's representative should expect to make three calls per sale.
Jerry Hay, manufacturer's rep, Burlington, Iowa

JON REIS

282. COMPARING A DOG'S AGE TO A HUMAN'S AGE   The
old rule — multiply a dog's real age by seven to find the equivalent human age — is fallacious. A dog is able to reproduce at one
year and has reached full growth by two years. To calculate a
dog's age in human terms, count the first year as fifteen, the second as ten, and each year after that as five.
Pierce Butler, Natchez, Mississippi

283. MEASURING THE NIGHT SKY   The moon covers half a
degree of sky.   *Tom Robinson, computer programmer, Berkeley, California*

284. DOING SOMETHING FOR MONEY   If someone says,
"It's not the money, it's the principle," it's really the money.
Dr. Angelo Valenti, consulting psychologist, Nashville, Tennessee

285. CONTROLLING YOURSELF   If you say, "I'll hate myself
in the morning for doing this," you're probably right.
Dr. Angelo Valenti, consulting psychologist, Nashville, Tennessee

286. PREDICTING BEHAVIOR   The best predictor of future
behavior is past behavior.
Dr. Angelo Valenti, consulting psychologist, Nashville, Tennessee

287. TAKING A MULTIPLE-CHOICE TEST   Don't change
your first guess on a multiple-choice question when checking over
your answers. The first guess is always the best.
William H. Smith, Cincinnati, Ohio

288. TAKING A MULTIPLE-CHOICE TEST   1. If you think
long — you think wrong. 2. Nine out of ten times, your first answer is the correct one. 3. When in doubt, pick answer C.
Robert Hastings, master chief petty officer, U.S. Coast Guard

289. TAKING A MULTIPLE-CHOICE TEST When in doubt, pick D on a multiple-choice test. *Cindy Watanabe, Honolulu, Hawaii*

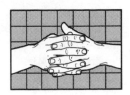

290. FRYING DONUTS When a film of smoke begins to rise from the hot fat, it is the right temperature for frying donuts. *Helen Ward, Cincinnati, Ohio*

291. WATERING YOUR GARDEN A newly prepared bed is properly watered if the shiny layer of excess water disappears within one-half to three seconds after you stop watering. One way to check if you have watered enough is to go out the next morning and poke your finger into the bed. If the soil is evenly moist for the first two inches and continues to be moist below this level, you are watering properly. If the soil is dry for part or all of the first two inches, you need more "shiny time." If the soil is soggy in part or all of the top two inches, you need less "shiny time." *John Jeavons, author of How to Grow More Vegetables*

292. PRICING A NIGHTCLUB In a bar or nightclub, when the lights go down, the prices go up. *Lori Edwards, Frederick, Maryland*

293. RUNNING A BOOTH AT A TRADE SHOW An industrious salesperson working a booth at a trade show should be able to chat briefly with about one hundred people per day. Ten percent of those people are likely to be good leads. *Allen Konopacki, president, Incomm International, in Business Week*

294. MAKING RUNWAYS OUT OF ICE Arctic engineers make their own icebergs to use as runways. It takes twenty-six inches of manmade ice to support a Caterpillar grader, five feet to support a 737 jet. Homemade ice forms faster and harder when the water is sprayed rather than flooded, but if the stream is aimed too high, the water falls as snow. *John Urquhart, staff reporter, Wall Street Journal, quoting Larry Sagriff, ice engineer, Panarctic Oils, Ltd., of Calgary*

295. PROVIDING WATER FOR FAMILIES A family of four uses roughly one acre-foot of water per year — that's the amount of water it takes to cover one acre of land with a foot of water. *William R. Doerner, Time*

296. FEEDING SOLDIERS WITH SNAILS Napoleon's troops carried canned snails as emergency rations. They allotted one thousand snails per soldier per week. *Michael McRae, Harrowsmith*

297. THE ONE-IN-FIVE RULE OF BUILDERS One in five building companies survives for fifteen years; one in five fails within five years. *Rick Eckstrom, builder, Danby, New York*

DEDE HATCH

298. HEATING AN AQUARIUM   To determine the proper wattage for an aquarium heater, allow three watts per gallon in a room at normal temperature. Use four watts per gallon for a room that is cooler than normal.   *Mary Ellen Parker, teacher, Cincinnati, Ohio*

299. MAKING A DEADLINE   When faced with a deadline, if you first tackle what *must* be done, then plan to do what *should* be done, saving for last what would be *nice* to do, you will seldom get past the first category. However, do those same things in reverse order, and somehow they will all get done, often with time to spare.   *Isabel T. Coburn, authority at large, Pemaquid Beach, Maine*

300. CLEANING UP LITTER   When a state passes a bottle bill, paper and plastic litter disappears from roadsides and parks in the same proportion that beverage bottles and cans do — which is almost totally.
Isabel T. Coburn, authority at large, Pemaquid Beach, Maine

301. REACHING A COMPROMISE   You know you've reached a good compromise if both sides are dissatisfied.
Thomas O. Marsh, writer and former charter commission chairman, Fairfield, Ohio

302. PLACING YOUR NAME ON A BALLOT   In a political race where none of the candidates is well known, the name listed first on the ballot (typically the names are in alphabetical order) has a major advantage.   *Pierce Butler, Natchez, Mississippi*

303. LISTENING TO CHICKADEES The warm weather of spring has finally arrived when the chickadees change their cry from *chick a dee dee dee* to *dee dee*.
Ronald and Christine Newberry, Cayutaville, New York

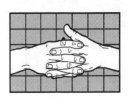

304. PUMPING BLOOD Your heart pushes about five tablespoons of blood into your arteries with each beat.
L. M. Boyd, San Francisco Chronicle

305. CHOOSING A FOREIGN RESTAURANT When traveling in a foreign country, avoid restaurants with menus printed in more than two languages — they are for tourists.
Michael Rider, art director, Ithaca, New York

306. THE DEATH RULE OF TWO In a geriatric patient population, twice as many people will die within the two months after their birthday as during any other two month period. One half as many will die within the two months before their birthday.
Gerry M. Flick, M.D., ship's surgeon, S.S. Constitution

307. GROWING TALLER A girl will reach her full height eighteen months after she starts to menstruate.
Hilary Peterson, homemaker, West Chester, Pennsylvania

308. BILLING A GOVERNMENT AGENCY When doing business with a government agency, expect to wait a minimum of 45 days to get paid, and don't get excited if it takes 90 to 120 days.
Scott M. Kruse, biogeographer, Fresno, California

309. DETERMINING YOUR FRAME SIZE To determine the size of your frame, wrap a dollar bill around your wrist. If the ends of the bill touch, you have a small frame. If there's a finger's width or less between then, you have a medium frame. Anything more than a finger's width and you have a large frame.
Scott Parker, Beaumont, Texas

310. WORKING WITH MASS TRANSIT When a mass transit system hikes fares by 10 percent, ridership usually declines permanently by 3 percent.
Joseph Schofer, transportation authority, quoted in In These Times

311. FENDING OFF A PUSHY SALESPERSON If you decide not to buy something, a pushy salesperson will often press you for a reason. The best response is, "I just don't know." If you give a specific reason, most salespeople will have a carefully planned retort. If you can't give them a reason, they can't give you an argument. *Phil A. Schrodt, associate professor, Northwestern University*

312. PLANTING BY THE MOON Plant root crops at the full moon. Above-ground crops should be planted at the new moon.
Larry Beck, joiner, Lansing, New York

JON CRISPIN

313. RAISING YOUR CHILDREN Parents teach more by example than by words. Reading parents have reading children; achieving parents have achieving children.
Denis Smith, school counselor, Camarillo, California

314. SIZING LUMBER Standard framing lumber spaced on sixteen-inch centers will span a distance, in feet, that is twice its wider dimension, in inches. For example, a two-by-eight will span sixteen feet. *Larry Beck, joiner, Lansing, New York*

315. INVESTING IN STOCKS   An average stock portfolio will outperform an average bond portfolio over time.
Phil Smith, Alameda, California

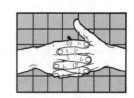

316. INVESTING IN MUTUAL FUNDS   In most cases, mutual fund managers and their funds will outperform your own portfolio.   *Phil Smith, Alameda, California*

317. SELECTING INVESTMENTS   When selecting investments, unwarranted conservatism, sloth, and inertia will outweigh logic and careful study about 50 percent of the time. Avarice, ignorance, and greed will outweigh logic and careful study about 15 percent of the time.   *Phil Smith, Alameda, California*

318. ATTRACTING HONEYBEES   Red flowers usually are ignored by honeybees; blue flowers usually attract them.
Pierce Butler, Natchez, Mississippi

319. LOSING BODY HEAT   Sixty percent of your body heat is lost through your head.   *Scott Parker, Beaumont, Texas*

320. MAKING A NEW CUSTOMER   Regardless of the product or the type of business, about one in three sales calls is to a new customer, and considering all expenses — salaries, commissions, benefits, travel, advertising, and follow-up calls — it costs about $1,500 to close a sale.
Elisabeth Colford, Cahners Publishing Company, Des Plaines, Illinois

321. SIZING UP A TEACHER   A teacher who complains that his or her students are all stupid is probably a poor teacher.
Bruce Reznick, associate professor of mathematics, Urbana, Illinois

322. GETTING RICH QUICK   The expectation of quick riches from investing is inversely proportional to the investor's knowledge of the markets and risk.   *Phil Smith, Alameda, California*

323. LOOKING AT BOOKS IN BOULDER   In any batch of fiction books, there will be more books by authors whose last names begin with *M* than any other letter. *S* will be second.
Ellen Klaver, musician, Boulder, Colorado

324. PLANNING A CLASS PARTY   If you teach in an elementary school and you are going to have a class party you should (1) have it on a day when there is no school the next day, (2) have it during the last period of the day, and (3) never have it last more than one hour.
Leonard F. Ferretti, elementary school teacher, Miami, Florida

Your portraits won't look so gimpy if you check to be sure the eyes are on a line halfway between the top of the head and the chin; the inside corners of the eyes are one eye-width apart; the nose is almost halfway between the eyes and chin; the nose is as wide as the distance between the eyes; the corners of the mouth fall directly below the pupils of the eyes; the tops of the ears are on eye level; and the bottoms of the ears come between the bottom of the nose and the mouth.

Alex Stewart, Atlanta, Georgia

325. SETTING THE PRICE OF A BOOK   When pricing a nonfiction book, estimate the cost of producing the first printing (including royalties), then set a tentative list price that will allow you to make a 20 percent pretax profit if the first printing sells.
Richard A. Balkin, Coda: Poets and Writers Newsletter

326. REMEMBERING A BOOK   For every worthwhile book you read there will be one statement or story you'll remember for a decade or longer.   *Scott Parker, Beaumont, Texas*

327. FIELDING A FLY BALL   If you play center field, wear a billed cap and keep your head level. Go in on a fly ball that does not disappear over the top of the bill; go out on any ball that disappears over the bill. If the ball is hit high and shallow, you will have time to recover.   *Henning Pape-Santos, linguist, New York City*

328. GUESSING A MAN'S AGE   To guess a man's age, take his height and multiply it by the number of times a day he goes to the bathroom.   *Henning Pape-Santos, linguist, New York City*

329. COOKING FISH   Broil fish ten minutes per inch of thickness.   *Michael Rider, art director, Ithaca, New York*

330. SMOKING IN THE DARK   If you enjoy smoking in the dark, it will be harder for you to give up cigarettes than someone who smokes only in daylight or well-lit rooms.
Gerry M. Flick, M.D., ship's surgeon, S.S. Constitution

331. TURNING A SHIP A deep-draft ship makes a 180-degree turn (or course reversal) in about the same length of time it takes to completely smoke a king-size cigarette.
John Towle, Salinas, California

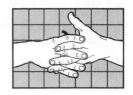

332. SHORTENING YOUR LIFE WITH CIGARETTES Each cigarette you smoke shortens your life by the amount of time you took to smoke it plus ten minutes.
Gerry M. Flick, M.D., ship's surgeon, S.S. Constitution

333. BUILDING A CAR Painting accounts for nearly half the cost of automobile assembly. *Scott Parker, Beaumont, Texas*

334. SHOPPING FOR PARKING A shopping mall should have 5.5 parking spaces for every one thousand square feet of gross leasable area. *Darryl Thomas, Rochester, New York*

335. RATING A MALL Any shopping mall with gross sales over $200 a square foot is a major success.
Darryl Thomas, Rochester, New York

336. GROWING MESQUITE It takes 1,725 pounds of water to grow one pound of mesquite, as opposed to only 705 pounds of water for one pound of side oats grama, the best grass for cattle. There have been cases where dry creeks have begun to flow again after mesquite was removed. *Robert Reinhold, writer, New York Times*

337. GETTING QUOTES ON A PRINTING JOB If a job is more than 10 percent of the year's printing budget, get six quotes. For smaller jobs, get three.
Camilla Walter, advertising manager, Ithaca, New York

338. CHECKING URINE As a rough estimate of how well hydrated a person is, or as one indicator of high sugar level in a diabetic, look at the urine. The darker the color, the higher the specific gravity, the greater the concentration of solutes, and the less hydrated the person is.
Scott M. Kruse, biogeographer, and Martha Betcher, medical technologist, Fresno, California

339. BIRD WATCHING You will hear one-third to one-half again as many chickadees and juncos as you will actually see, and there are one-third again as many out there that you neither hear nor see. *Ellen Klaver, musician, Boulder, Colorado*

340. CHOOSING A SURGICAL ASSISTANT If you are a surgeon, choose an assistant surgeon whose height is within five inches of yours. Otherwise, you will disagree on the height of the operating table, and if the operation is long, one of you will end up with back pain. *Gerry M. Flick, M.D., ship's surgeon, S.S. Constitution*

When you use the time-out method to discipline a child, use one minute for each year of the child's age.

John Fischer, Joliet, Montana

341. ENTERING THE GROUND CUSHION   The ground cushion is an invisible area above the runway where the interaction between the airplane's wing and the ground causes changes in an airplane's flight characteristics. Measured scientifically, the height of the ground cushion is about equal to the wingspan of the airplane. A pilot, however, will notice the effects at an altitude equal to half the wingspan of the airplane.
Richard L. Collins, editor in chief, Flying

342. LANDING AN AIRPLANE   To make every landing as much the same as possible, enter the ground cushion with the airplane trimmed to 1.2 to 1.3 times its stalling speed.
Richard L. Collins, editor in chief, Flying

343. COUNTING YOUR VOLUNTEERS   Any volunteer organization is alive and well if at least 35 percent of its members volunteer consistently.   *John Towle, Salinas, California*

344. FOLLOWING BUBBLES   When scuba diving, don't rise to the surface any faster than the smallest bubbles you exhale.
Alex Stewart, Atlanta, Georgia

345. SCUBA DIVING IN SHALLOW WATER   You don't need to worry about decompression stops if you scuba-dive at depths of thirty feet or less.   *Alex Stewart, Atlanta, Georgia*

346. PLANNING SIDEWALKS   To determine where the sidewalks for a new building on campus should be, construct the building without sidewalks and wait for one year. Then put sidewalks on the paths the students have made.
Larry Morgan and Fred Fry, Kansas City, Missouri

347. WORRYING ABOUT BLOOD PRESSURE   The systolic (top) pressure for an adult male under forty should be his age plus one hundred. For an adult female, it's her age plus ninety.
Dennis Pollack, builder, Danby, New York

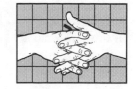

348. WAITING FOR RAIN   If there's dew on the spider webs in the grass in the morning, it won't rain.
Pete Stewart, auctioneer, Armagh, Pennsylvania

349. CHECKING SPIDER WEBS FOR DEW   If in the evening you can find beads of dew on spider webs, the next day will bring good, dry haying weather.   *Retired dairy farmer, Albany, Vermont*

350. CHECKING THE GRASS FOR DEW   Brush your hand over the grass well after sunset. If it is dry, the next day will be too wet for haying.   *Retired dairy farmer, Albany, Vermont*

351. WAITING FOR THE FIRST FROST   The first frost will come six weeks after you hear the last cricket.
Fred Brehm, vegetable grower, Dilltown, Pennsylvania

352. BUYING CHAMPAGNE   Always buy one more bottle of champagne than you think you'll need for every four people.
David Nowicki, wine authority, Interlaken, New York

353. THE THREE-CASE RULE   Be methodical about accumulating wine in your cellar. If you can manage to get three cases ahead, you can stop worrying about having a good supply.
David Nowicki, wine authority, Interlaken, New York

354. ESTIMATING YOUR STRIDE   When you walk, your leg length is equal to the length of your stride.
Ned Frederick, writer, Exeter, New Hampshire

355. FIXING YOUR CAR   If a car that was working stops or won't start, the problem is probably simple to fix. Catastrophic failures of major parts are rare. The apparent frequency of major breakdowns is due to unscrupulous or lazy repair shops, which don't look for the simple solutions, and the publicity surrounding auto racing, where catastrophic failure is more common.
Phil A. Schrodt, associate professor, Northwestern University

356. LOOKING AT PEPPER GRINDERS   The quality of food at a restaurant is inversely proportional to the size of the pepper grinders.
Morris J. Markovitz, A. C. Israel Enterprises, White Plains, New York

357. CALLING SOMEONE UP   If you are a single woman, never call a person with whom you have a sexually ambiguous relationship when you are drunk.
Ruth Anne Schultz, rain check coordinator, Kingston, Massachusetts

On Friday and Saturday nights, one in ten cars coming toward you has a drunk driver behind the wheel.

Scott Parker, Beaumont, Texas, quoting Parade

JON REIS

358. WATCHING THE SUN SET IN OAKLAND It takes two minutes for the sun to drop out of sight once it touches the horizon. *Emmon Bodfish, Oakland, California*

359. EMMON'S RULE OF BREATHING When you're relaxed, you take approximately twelve breaths per minute.
Emmon Bodfish, Oakland, California

360. BETTING ON A HORSE   If you don't know any of the horses in a race, bet on the one with the thinnest waist.
Thomas O. Marsh, writer, Fairfield, Ohio

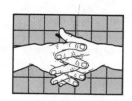

361. EXPLAINING COMPUTERS   When explaining a computer command, a computer language feature, or a piece of computer hardware, first describe the problem it is designed to solve.
David Martin, Norristown, Pennsylvania, in Communications of the ACM

362. LOOKING AT SPECKS   If your eyes can see it, you need to worry about it. That's the rule for any faint mark or strange speck on artwork headed for the printer. Otherwise, if you want something to show up, it won't. And if you don't want something to show up, it will.   *Michael Rider, art director, Ithaca, New York*

363. PLANNING A CAMPING TRIP   A camping trip is in jeopardy whenever early risers or night owls exceed 50 percent of the party. If either is a majority, the other campers should reassess their plans.   *Denis Smith, school counselor, Camarillo, California*

364. COMPARING MOVIES TO BOOKS   Comparing a movie to a book is easy when one inspired the other. The one created first will be better.   *Mark Alber, Houston, Texas*

365. SIZING UP AN EVANGELIST   An evangelist who quotes the Book of Romans is likely to be a Fundamentalist Christian.
Steven F. Scharff, cartoonist, Hillside Township, New Jersey

366. CHECKING A DRAWING   It's easier to check the proportions of a drawing if it's held upside down.
Steven F. Scharff, cartoonist, Hillside Township, New Jersey

367. RUNNING A LIGHT IN NEW JERSEY   New Jersey traffic lights have an amber signal lasting one second for every ten miles per hour of the posted speed limit.
Steven F. Scharff, cartoonist, Hillside Township, New Jersey

368. PUNISHING A CHILD   When you use the time-out method to discipline a child, impose one minute for each year of the child's age.   *John Fischer, Joliet, Montana*

369. WATCHING A TAKEOVER   When a company is taken over by another firm in the same field, and it was doing well before the takeover, it will do less well afterward. If it was not doing well before the takeover, its future will be about as murky as before — or a little more so.
Walter Pitkin, literary agent, Weston, Connecticut

> Generally speaking, if your cat nudges your feet in the morning, it wants to stay inside. If it nudges your face, it wants to go out.
>
> *Mark McMullen, accountant, Alexandria, Virginia*

JON REIS

370. CHECKING YOUR EAR LOBES   If your ear lobes have a diagonal crease, you may have clogged coronary arteries.
Joe Graedon, Medical Self-Care

371. CHECKING A BEER BELLY   Measure the circumference of your waist and hips. If your waist-to-hips ratio is over 1.0 (for men) or above 0.8 (for women), your risk of heart attack or stroke is five to ten times greater than if the ratio is lower.
US Pharmacist

372. DESIGNING A SUPERMARKET   Supermarket efficiency increases with store size to a maximum of 22,000 square feet. After that, economies of scale are offset by communication problems.   *Retail Management Letter*

373. CHOOSING A TENNIS RACQUET #1   If your tennis racquet twists in your hand, the grip is probably too small. If your arm tires from hanging on too tightly, the grip is too big.
Diversion, quoted in Bottom Line/Personal

374. CHOOSING A TENNIS RACQUET #2   To choose the right grip for a tennis racquet, measure the distance from the tip of your middle finger to the crease in the middle of your palm. That equals the right-size handle.
Dr. David Bachman, Tribune Media Services

375. SORTING OUT HOUSE NUMBERS Even-numbered houses typically can be found on the west and north sides of streets, odd-numbered houses on the east and south. Usually, house numbers change consecutively in even-number increments — in most cases it is four. In some cases it is either two or six, depending on the density of the neighborhood.
Bob Horton, consultant and writer, St. Petersburg, Florida

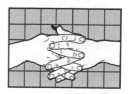

376. ASKING FOR PERMISSION It is generally easier to ask forgiveness than permission.
Andrea Frankel, computer scientist, quoting Grace Hopper, San Diego, California

377. CHOOSING A TIE A 3½-inch-wide tie will never go out of style. *John Green, Ann Arbor, Michigan*

378. ENTERING A CROWDED MOVIE THEATER When entering a crowded movie theater, more empty seats will be found on the aisle farthest from the entrance. If all the aisles are essentially straight ahead of the entrance, select the leftmost aisle — most people go to the right-hand aisles.
W. G. Martin, San Diego, California

379. FINDING A GOOD RESTAURANT ABROAD To find good restaurants in small towns abroad, ask the local butcher. He knows who buys the best cuts. *Travelore Reports*

380. CHOOSING A RESTAURANT Pick the restaurant with the most cars parked in front of it.
Mr. and Mrs. Edward Hughes, Arlington, Virginia

381. CHECKING YOUR SHOCKS To check your shock absorbers, bounce your car up and down with your foot on the bumper. If the car keeps on bouncing after you stop, you need new shocks. *Tom Robinson, computer programmer, Berkeley, California*

382. WORKING WITH PURCHASING AGENTS Most firms change 20 to 25 percent of their suppliers every year.
Scott Parker, Beaumont, Texas

383. BUYING IMPORTED BEER When buying imported beer, you pay about $1 a six-pack in taxes.
Dave Graham, engineer and authority on beer

384. BETSY'S OVERLOOKED RULE Two's company, three's a crowd. *Betsy Cook, composer, Buckinghamshire, England*

385. OPERATING A RESTAURANT If a customer likes your restaurant, he'll tell two other people. If a customer hates your restaurant, he'll tell seven other people. *Jeff Hamilton, ex-waiter*

> If your fiancé does something that bothers you before you're married, it will bother you ten times more after you're married.

Bruno Colapietro, matrimonial lawyer with over eight thousand cases, Binghamton, New York

386. USING PUBLIC WASHROOMS In a public washroom, always use the toilet farthest away from the door. It is normally cleaner and less used than the ones closer to the door.
Tony Campo, Jr., sales rep for food service equipment, Countryside, Illinois

387. HANDLING AN IN-FLIGHT EMERGENCY When in doubt, fly low and slow; when in extreme doubt, kick top rudder. *Ray Pineo, fly fisherman and retired pilot, Newville, Pennsylvania*

388. THE CATERER'S RULE When planning a party, figure three pieces per person of whatever you're serving.
Shelby Herman, economist

389. SIZING-UP SOMEONE The more a person tries to come across in a certain way, the less likely that he feels that way about himself. In other words, the bigger the bully, the more insecure he feels.
Drs. Kim and Jack Arthur, child psychotherapists, Baltimore, Maryland

390. SELLING STRAWBERRY SHORTCAKE Rectangular servings of strawberry shortcake sell better than round servings. *L. M. Boyd, San Francisco Chronicle*

391. CLEANING ANTIQUE WEAPONS Anything a novice does to improve the looks of an antique weapon probably will lower its value or destroy it as a collector's piece.
Jim Barber, historian and collector, Springfield, Missouri

392. SHOPPING IN A THIRD WORLD COUNTRY #1 When you shop in a Third World market, start by offering the seller half the asking price, then settle on about three-quarters. If the seller doesn't adhere to this rule — if he accepts your initial offer of one half — then you are being taken.
Phil A. Schrodt, associate professor, Northwestern University

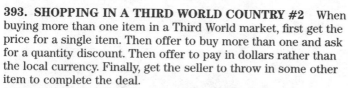

393. SHOPPING IN A THIRD WORLD COUNTRY #2 When buying more than one item in a Third World market, first get the price for a single item. Then offer to buy more than one and ask for a quantity discount. Then offer to pay in dollars rather than the local currency. Finally, get the seller to throw in some other item to complete the deal.
Phil A. Schrodt, associate professor, Northwestern University

394. LOCATING WILDERNESS In the western United States, any area that has more than one mile of road per one thousand acres will have a tough time gaining congressional protection as a wilderness area. *Henning Pape-Santos, linguist, New York City*

395. PRESERVING YOUR SHOES Shoes last half again as long if you keep them in their shoe box when you aren't wearing them. *Kirstin Hark, seventh grade student, Conroe, Texas*

396. CRISPIN'S RULE OF PHYSICAL WELL-BEING If you piss light, you're all right. *Jon Crispin, photographer, Ithaca, New York*

397. WEIGHING A LETTER If you need to know whether your letter weighs less than an ounce, compare it with the weight of five quarters. For two ounces, use five half dollars.
Denis Smith, school counselor, Camarillo, California

398. DIAGNOSING A PATIENT Seventy percent of medical diagnoses can be made by taking a good medical history. Another 20 percent can be made by doing a good physical exam. Only 10 percent require laboratory procedures and X-rays.
Gerry M. Flick, M.D., ship's surgeon, S.S. Constitution

399. MAILING FORMS TO EMPLOYEES For every 150 W-2 forms you mail to employees at the end of the year, you should expect four or five returns. They'll need new addresses, corrections, or better carbon copies.
Jackie Creble, secretary, Burlington, Iowa

400. SPOTTING A CITY SLICKER Never trust a man who parts his hair in the middle or his name on the side.
John Bailey, Deer Lick Farm, Interlaken, New York

401. CHOOSING A TYPESETTER When using an inexpensive typesetter, plan on at least five return visits to get it right.
Alan Hoffman, creative director, Digicomp Research, Ithaca, New York

JON REIS

402. MONITORING YOUR UNBORN BABY If your unborn baby kicks less than ten times in twelve hours, call your doctor immediately. You should also consult the doctor if the tenth movement is coming later each day. *Jay Butera, writer, American Health*

403. THE BAFFLING RULE OF PLANTING OATS Plant your oats when the shad is in the blow.
Steve Sierigk, artist, Ithaca, New York

404. NEGOTIATING AN AGREEMENT When negotiating, use a deadline. Ninety percent of the agreement will come in the last 10 percent of the time allotted.
Lory Peck, social worker, Albany, New York

405. RECUPERATING For every day you spend in the hospital, plan on one week to recuperate.
Jon Crispin, photographer, Ithaca, New York

406. CLAIMING YOUR MEDICAL INSURANCE If you're fully insured, you will spend two full days doing insurance paperwork to cover seven days in the hospital.
John E. Harney, Concord, New Hampshire

407. EXTENDING CREDIT Republicans always pay their bills. Democrats don't. *Anonymous landlord, Albany, New York*

408. DESIGNING A RELIEF MAP A relief map needs to have its vertical proportions exaggerated by a factor of two.
Peter Reimuller, Point Arena, California

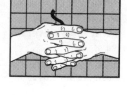

409. ESTIMATING THE DISTANCE OF AN OBJECT To estimate the distance between you and a distant object, close one eye and look over the thumb of your outstretched arm, fixing a point on the object. Close the other eye and open the first one. Your thumb will be fixed on another point near the object. Estimate the distance between these two points and multiply by seven. This will give you the approximate distance from you to the object. *Wolf Juckoff, former German boy scout, Rexville, New York*

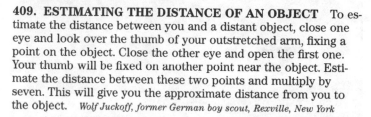

410. ADDRESSING ENVELOPES The average person can attach 400 to 450 pressure-sensitive address labels to envelopes per hour. Someone who is very fast can do 800.
David Updike, president, The Mail Box of Ithaca, Ithaca, New York

411. PLANNING A LONG RUN Plan to do your longest training runs on an empty stomach, beginning before eight A.M. For each hour after eight that you begin, cut the distance by 10 percent. Add 10 percent if you have one or two cups of coffee before starting. *Tom Ferguson, M.D., editor, Medical Self-Care*

412. GETTING TICKETS TO A PLAY In bad weather, you can always get a seat or two for any play — and the no-show seats are generally better than the ones your friends got by ordering weeks in advance.
Kelly Yeaton, teacher and stage manager, State College, Pennsylvania

413. GETTING A QUICK ANSWER You'll spend less time getting answers from people if you go to their offices to ask them questions. That way, you control when the conversation ends.
Dean Sheridan, Downey, California

414. ILLUSTRATING YOUR DATA If your data include fewer than twenty pieces of information, a graphic presentation is unnecessary.
Edward R. Tufte, author of The Visual Display of Quantitative Information

415. FEELING THE FLIES If flies bite, it will rain.
Johnnie Putnam, WIND radio, Chicago, Illinois

416. WORKING FOR TIPS The best tippers are men dining with their dates — not with their wives.
Johnnie Putnam, WIND radio, Chicago, Illinois

417. PAPERING A WALL When papering an average wall with a print or striped wallpaper, expect to lose at least one foot of paper per floor-to-ceiling strip to match the pattern.
Johnnie Putnam, WIND radio, Chicago, Illinois

Children aged six to ten outgrow their shoes every 84 days.

Mason Speed, WTKO radio, Ithaca, New York

418. ACCEPTING A BLIND DATE When a matchmaking friend describes a potential date as "sweet, friendly, and intelligent," you can be sure he or she won't be much to look at. This is true even when you are hoping it might be an exception.
Johnnie Putnam, WIND radio, Chicago, Illinois

419. THE ENTERTAINER'S RULE #1 Look good, sound good, and do something good. To make a steady living, you need all three. To be on television, you can get away with only two.
Timothy Wenk, magician, West Stockbridge, Massachusetts

420. THE ENTERTAINER'S RULE #2 Always dress one step better than the best-dressed person in your audience. If he is wearing jeans, for example, you should wear a suit; if a suit, then a tux. *Timothy Wenk, magician, West Stockbridge, Massachusetts*

421. THE ENTERTAINER'S RULE #3 You should spend about four times your fee for a single gig on a suit or dress for your performance, and one night's fee on the shoes.
Timothy Wenk, magician, West Stockbridge, Massachusetts

422. DECIDING WHAT YOU WANT If you don't know what you want, it's probably sleep.
Timothy Wenk, magician, West Stockbridge, Massachusetts

423. DECIDING WHAT TO EAT If you can't figure out what you want to eat, you're not hungry.
Andrea Frankel, computer scientist, engineer, and holistic health practitioner, San Diego, California

424. USING A FUTON It takes two futons to make a comfortable bed. *Steve Keast, hazard investigator, Slaterville Springs, New York*

425. SOLICITING PAPERS FROM STUDENTS In a college classroom, roughly 10 percent of the term papers will be handed in late. Increasing the penalty for a late paper has no effect on this statistic unless more than one term paper is required.
Phil A. Schrodt, associate professor, Northwestern University

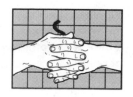

426. CHANGING YOUR SEX A male who changes his sex will look like a woman who is five years older because men's faces look more rugged than women's. On the other hand, female-to-male sex-change patients will look ten to twelve years younger. A thirty-year-old woman will look and sound like a man of eighteen or twenty. It's called the "Peter Pan effect."
Marge Willes, counselor, Gateway Gender Alliance

427. GAUGING THE SPEED OF ANOTHER BOAT To gauge the speed of another boat that is moving in the same direction as yours, choose a point on the horizon that is behind the other boat and check how the boat's bow moves relative to this point. If its bow appears to move ahead of the point, the other boat is moving faster than yours; if its bow appears to move backward, your boat is going faster. If there is no relative movement, and your boats are on intersecting courses, you're in for a collision.
Evan Gamblin, Carleton Place, Ontario

428. FOLLOWING FASHIONS When a popular phenomenon reaches the cover of *Time*, it is already out of fashion.
Richard L. Holloway, associate professor, University of Minnesota

429. SWATTING BOTHERSOME FLIES Wait for a fly to land. Sneak up from behind and clap your hands together one or two inches directly above the fly. Flies always fly straight up first when making a getaway. With practice, you'll clap the fly nine times out of ten.
M. J. T. Ferguson, retired taxi driver, Narberth, Pennsylvania

430. WAITING FOR SNOW 'Twon't snow till the brooks flow.
Clem Braczyk, quoting George, an old woodcutter, Webster, Massachusetts

431. GIVING A SPEECH A good speech will present one idea per five-minute period, but no more than two or three ideas in a twenty-minute talk. *Robert Prescott, writer, USAir*

432. KISSING SOMEONE If a man's a good kisser, he's a great f——. *Cher, quoted in People*

433. ALPHABETIZING THINGS Twenty-five percent of any alphabetical list will be under the first three letters of the alphabet. *Lewy Olfson, contemplative, Stonington, Connecticut*

434. THE JAPANESE RULE OF FLOWER ARRANGING   Put into the vase one-third as many flowers as you think you need, then take half of them out.
Lewy Olfson, contemplative, Stonington, Connecticut

435. CONSULTING   A consultant should spend two-thirds of his or her time consulting with clients and one-third lining up new work and doing PR.
Peter K. Francese, president, American Demographics, Inc., Ithaca, New York

436. COOKING VEGETABLES   Cook vegetables the way they grow: Cook roots covered, starting them in cold water. Cook greens uncovered in boiling water.
Kelly Yeaton, quoting "The Mystery Chef," a 1930s radio cooking show

437. WORKING WITH GROUPS   Twenty percent of any group will be critical of the rest.   *Marilyn Rider, Ithaca, New York*

438. FOLLOWING FALL   On the East Coast of the United States, the fall foliage change moves south by fifty miles a day.
Margaret Wagner, Brooklyn, New York

439. CHECKING YOUR MUSSELS   Squeeze a mussel. If it doesn't stay shut, it's dead.   *Margaret Wagner, Brooklyn, New York*

440. STARTING A NEW BUSINESS   Do not start a new business unless you can wait at least one year before realizing a profit.   *Thomas O. Marsh, writer, Fairfield, Ohio*

441. ROB'S RULE OF SLUSHES   Never drink a slush or a slurpee fast or you will get a fifteen-second headache.
Rob Frank, Saginaw, Michigan

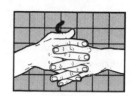

442. HITCHING HORSES   When you're hitching horses, the double tree or evener should be the same length as the neck yoke.   *Fr. Emmet C. Smith, Largo, Florida*

443. WINNING THE HEARTS OF YOUR PARISH   The first year the parish loves you, the second year they hate you, the third year they understand you.   *Fr. Emmet C. Smith, Largo, Florida*

444. FEELING YOUR AGE   You are middle aged when your high school and college days are featured as nostalgia on TV. You are old when your wedding presents are sold as antiques.
Margaret M. Day, Locke, New York

445. LOOKING FOR ENGINEERING CORRELATIONS   If you are trying to describe a phenomenon rigorously, correlate aggregate parameters in such a way that all the units cancel out. For example, don't study the effect of changing pipe diameter, which has units of distance. Study changes of pipe diameter divided by pipe length, which has units of distance divided by distance. The result is dimensionless. These correlations are more resilient to changes in materials and scale.
David R. Throop, chemical engineer, Austin, Texas

446. QUICKLY CHECKING A BOOK   A good way to get the "feel" of a book is to read the table of contents, then read the index, if it has one, and finally read the first and last paragraphs of each chapter.   *Bob Horton, consultant and writer, St. Petersburg, Florida*

447. WATCHING A MARRIAGE #1   Each $1,000 raise in a wife's earnings increases the chance of divorce or separation by 1 percent.   *Lory Peck, social worker, Albany, New York*

448. WATCHING A MARRIAGE #2   The lower the wife's income, the more likely she and her husband will reconcile.
Lory Peck, social worker, Albany, New York

449. WATCHING A MARRIAGE #3   Men who have unstable employment histories are twice as likely to separate from their wives as those who have steady jobs.
Lory Peck, social worker, Albany, New York

450. WATCHING A MARRIAGE #4   For each year in a person's life that marriage is delayed, the chances of separating fall by 1 percent.   *Lory Peck, social worker, Albany, New York*

Four hugs a day is the minimum needed to meet a person's "skin hunger."

Greg Risberg, clinical social worker, North-western University Medical School

451. WALKING AND BACKPACKING At a steady, unhurried pace, you can walk three miles per hour without a backpack and one mile per hour with a heavy backpack.
Peter Reimuller, Point Arena, California

452. APPROACHING A BIRD The smaller the bird, the closer it will allow you to approach.
Thomas O. Marsh, writer and bird watcher, Fairfield, Ohio

453. RUNNING GUNS Plan on spending $125,000 on weapons for each enemy soldier you need to kill in a war.
Scott Parker, Beaumont, Texas

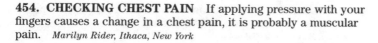

454. CHECKING CHEST PAIN If applying pressure with your fingers causes a change in a chest pain, it is probably a muscular pain. *Marilyn Rider, Ithaca, New York*

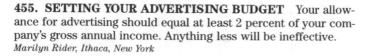

455. SETTING YOUR ADVERTISING BUDGET Your allowance for advertising should equal at least 2 percent of your company's gross annual income. Anything less will be ineffective.
Marilyn Rider, Ithaca, New York

456. GETTING SOMETHING DONE If you want something done, give it to a busy person. *Scott Parker, Beaumont, Texas*

457. WATCHING BIRDS Study the bird, not the field guide. The bird will fly away, the guide won't.
Christine Jones, bird watcher, San Francisco, California

458. LOOKING AT BIRD BILLS The single best clue to a bird's identity is the shape of its bill.
Christine Jones, bird watcher, San Francisco, California

459. LOOKING FOR BIRDS Look for birds on the edges where two habitats meet — ocean beaches, sides of streams, forest margins. There you can find organisms from both habitats, plus those adapted to the edge itself.
Christine Jones, bird watcher, San Francisco, California

460. MANAGING SALESPEOPLE You can fire half of all the salespeople in the country and never notice a drop in sales.
Vince Mooney, real estate broker, Tulsa, Oklahoma

461. RESEARCHING A BUSINESS VENTURE When you are researching a venture capital project, speak to at least twenty-five people, twenty of whom were not suggested by the entrepreneur.
Scott Parker, Beaumont, Texas, quoting George Weller, attorney and venture capital consultant

462. DEALING WITH DOUBT (PERSONAL CLARITY) If you are a masseuse, counselor, or other therapist, when in doubt, reschedule your client. Going through with a session when you are "processing your own stuff" will cause you to lose the client; rescheduling won't.
Andrea Frankel, computer scientist, engineer, and holistic health practitioner, San Diego, California

463. THE CARPENTRY RULE Customers give carpenters the hardest time on the smallest jobs.
Antonio V. Farulla, carpenter, Sherman Oaks, California

464. BUILDING A HOUSE   Sixty percent of the construction costs for a frame house are labor, 40 percent are materials.
J. Johnson, Fort Collins, Colorado

465. HOLDING A JOB   The more you need your job for financial reasons, the worse you will be treated.
J. Johnson, Fort Collins, Colorado

466. ADJUSTING WHEEL BEARINGS   Tighten the wheel bearing nut until there is no slop, then back it up one-eighth turn.   *Garry Harned, authority on frog communication, Ithaca, New York*

467. CALL IN BARTENDERS   When you're scheduling bartenders for a college-town bar, figure that twenty-five hard-drinking townies equal seventy-five students.   *Cheryl Plumb, Ithaca, New York*

468. LISTENING TO SNOW   Snow squeaks when the temperature is below 20° F.
Thomas Lack, somewhere on the east shore of Lake Michigan

469. WATCHING YOUR BREATH   When you see your breath, the temperature is below 45° F.
Thomas Lack, somewhere on the east shore of Lake Michigan

470. COUNTING GUNSHOTS   If you hear shots while hunting: One shot equals game bagged. Two shots equals game possibly bagged. Three shots means there's a chance game was bagged. Four shots means you're listening to a frustrated hunter.
Thomas Lack, somewhere on the east shore of Lake Michigan

471. FINDING A BALL IN THE ROUGH   To find a golf ball, first look ten yards past where you think you hit it out, then look ten yards short, and finally five yards farther into the rough.
Michael D. Miles, Aloha, Oregon

472. GETTING TO THE GREEN   To hit a ball to the green, first decide which club will get it to the green with your best swing, then swallow your pride and use the next longest club and a more relaxed swing. (Instead of a five iron, use a four iron.) You'll be on the green far more often than you'll be over it. The ball will fly straighter too.   *Michael D. Miles, Aloha, Oregon*

473. WORKING WITH ELECTRICAL ENGINEERS   The finished product will usually draw 50 percent more power than the electrical engineer estimated when he or she designed the circuit.   *Michael D. Miles, Aloha, Oregon*

474. SCHEDULING A CRUISE   Change the date of your cruise if over 5 percent of the other passengers have won the trip instead of paying for it out of their own pockets.
Gerry M. Flick, M.D., ship's surgeon, S.S. Constitution

475. WATCHING WIND AND RAIN   Wind before rain, you'll be sailing again. Rain before wind, take your sails in.
Tim Slack, chief mate, S.S. Constitution

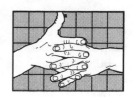

476. CHECKING A BOTTLE OF WINE   Be suspicious of any wine that does not have sediment or tannin crystals in it after ten or twelve years of aging.
Cally Arthur, managing editor, Alpine, New York

477. INSTALLING A KITCHEN SINK   Install a kitchen sink so that its bottom is at the same height as the hip bone of the tallest person using it. Everybody else can stand on little kick-away platforms.   *Fred Pape, Union City, California*

478. MIKE'S TEST FOR SILICONE   A woman has had silicone implants in her breasts if her nipples turn down.
Mike Garside, corrections officer, Ithaca, New York

479. SPENDING MONEY ON COMPUTERS   Average users of personal computers will spend as much on software as they did on the original machine. Sophisticated users will spend as much on additional hardware as they spent on the original machine, and twice as much on software.
Phil A. Schrodt, associate professor, Northwestern University

480. STARTING A FIRE   One stick can't burn; two sticks won't burn; three sticks might burn; four sticks will burn; five sticks make a nice fire.   *Gail Smith, parts unknown*

481. WHIPPING UP A CASSEROLE OR STEW   To make a casserole or stew without a recipe, use approximately equal volumes of all the main ingredients, and add double that volume of the main starch — rice, potatoes, noodles, etc.
Gail Smith, parts unknown

482. GETTING SOMEWHERE ON TIME   To make sure you get somewhere on time, double the estimated travel time for a trip of ten minutes or less; add fifteen minutes to a trip of thirty minutes or less; add fifty percent to a trip of one-half to two hours; and add 25 to 30 percent to a trip of more than two hours.   *Gail Smith, parts unknown*

483. MEASURING AN INFANT   The circumference of a normal infant's head should equal the distance from the crown of the head to the rump.
Thomas O. Marsh, writer and coroner's investigator, Fairfield, Ohio

DEDE HATCH

484. SHEDENHELM'S CRAZY RULE OF ROASTING   To
make sure that your roast chicken will be thoroughly done, mix a
handful of uncooked popcorn with the stuffing. Place the foil-
wrapped stuffed chicken in a 375-degree oven. In roughly an hour,
when the chicken explodes, the fragments will be tender and
juicy.   *W. R. C. Shedenhelm, chicken demolitionist, Encino, California*

485. PLANTING BARLEY   How much do you lose per acre by
planting your barley late? A bushel a day after the first of May.
Marty Schlabach, co-owner, Shelter Goods, Rochester, New York

486. WORKING WITH SPINNERS   It takes seven hand spinners to keep one weaver busy.
Jon Reis, photographer, overheard at a craft show in Ithaca, New York

487. KEEPING UP WITH MEDICINE   The half-life of knowledge in medical school is four years. Fifty percent of what you
learn as a freshman is obsolete when you graduate.
Dr. Lawrence Senterfit, microbiologist, Cornell Medical School

488. REMEMBERING WHAT YOU LEARNED   You will remember only 10 percent of what you think you learned in college.   *Isabel T. Coburn, authority at large, Pemaquid Beach, Maine*

489. WRITING A MAGAZINE ARTICLE   After your notes are
prepared and your outline is written, count on one hour of writing
time for every double-spaced typewritten page.
Brad Edmondson, writer, Ithaca, New York

490. BUILDING NURSING HOMES The United States needs to open one new nursing home per day for the rest of the century to keep up with the projected demand for geriatric care.
Brad Edmondson, writer, Ithaca, New York

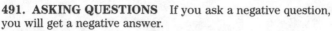

491. ASKING QUESTIONS If you ask a negative question, you will get a negative answer.
Denis Smith, school counselor, Camarillo, California

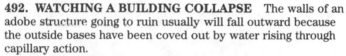

492. WATCHING A BUILDING COLLAPSE The walls of an adobe structure going to ruin usually will fall outward because the outside bases have been coved out by water rising through capillary action.
Chris Wilson, architectural historian, Albuquerque, New Mexico

493. BURNING CALORIES For every kilometer (six-tenths of a mile) you run, you burn one calorie per kilogram of your body weight. Swimming a kilometer requires about four calories per kilogram of body weight. Cycling a kilometer requires about one-third calorie per kilogram. *Ned Frederick, writer, Exeter, New Hampshire*

494. DETERMINING YOUR BASAL METABOLIC RATE
Your basal metabolic rate is equal to your weight in kilograms. For example, a person weighing sixty kilograms (132 pounds) burns about sixty calories per hour at rest.
Ned Frederick, writer, Exeter, New Hampshire

495. ATTRACTING A VENTURE CAPITALIST Venture capitalists invest in only about 3 percent of the deals that come across their desks each year. *Scott Parker, Beaumont, Texas*

496. PLANNING A MEETING A meeting without an agenda will take twice as long and accomplish half as much as a meeting with an agenda.
Andrea Frankel, computer scientist, engineer, and holistic health practitioner, San Diego, California

497. FUELING A TRUCK The average tractor-trailer gets four to five miles per gallon on the highway.
L. M. Boyd, San Francisco Chronicle

498. BRINGING IN THE INFIELD Here's an old baseball rule: When you bring in the infield, you make a .400 hitter out of a .200 hitter. *Henning Pape-Santos, linguist, New York City*

499. MICROWAVING VEGETABLES When microwaving solid vegetables, figure seven minutes per pound. This works on broccoli, cauliflower, carrots, winter squash, potatoes, yams, asparagus, cabbage, and other vegetables of similar density.
Andrea Frankel, computer scientist, engineer, and holistic health practitioner, San Diego, California

JON REIS

500. FINDING GOLDFISH There are at least two goldfish in every farm tank in the United States.
Mark Ellenburg, artist, New York City

501. FINDING FIREWOOD The best firewood comes from the tree that grows closest to the woodshed.
Alan H. Haeberle, Ithaca, New York, quoting Blair & Ketchum's Country Journal

502. SELECTING A NAIL Choose a nail that's 2½ to 3 times longer than the thickness of the piece of wood you want to nail.
Alan H. Haeberle, Ithaca, New York, quoting Blair & Ketchum's Country Journal

503. TESTING SUNGLASSES For high-altitude skiing, you need very dark sunglasses. With your sunglasses on, look in a bathroom mirror. If you can see your eyes, the glasses aren't dark enough. *Rick Eckstrom, builder, Danby, New York*

504. BLOCKING THE WIND A semipermeable row of plants will shelter the ground behind it for a distance of twenty times the height of the plants, whether they are ten inches or two hundred feet tall. For example, a shelter belt of sixty-foot poplars with a shrubbery understory will protect the soil downwind for twelve hundred feet — regardless of wind speed.
Pierce Butler, Natchez, Mississippi

505. WAITING FOR THE MOON The moon rises fifty minutes later than it did the day before. *Pierce Butler, Natchez, Mississippi*

506. SELLING EYEGLASSES You can figure that eight out of every ten people walking by your optical shop will need prescription eyeglasses by age forty-five.
Peter Potenza, optician, Ithaca, New York

507. PROMOTING A MOVIE Marketing and distribution costs for a movie run about 2½ times the film's production budget.
Scott Parker, Beaumont, Texas

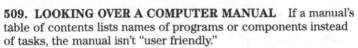

508. WATCHING DEER If you see deer feeding in the early afternoon, expect a change in the weather in twenty-four to forty-eight hours. *Glen Fritz, Burlington, Iowa*

509. LOOKING OVER A COMPUTER MANUAL If a manual's table of contents lists names of programs or components instead of tasks, the manual isn't "user friendly."
Bruce Nevin, editor and technical writer, Gloucester, Massachusetts

510. THE INTERSECTION RULE When the light turns green, it takes about as long for the car in front of you to start moving as it does for the traffic coming the other way to reach you.
Bruce Nevin, editor and technical writer, Gloucester, Massachusetts

511. WRITING A TECHNICAL MANUAL After the basic research is done, a technical manual takes about one hour to write and three hours to edit per page.
Bruce Nevin, editor and technical writer, Gloucester, Massachusetts

512. REACHING THE HORIZON The distance to the horizon, in miles, is the square root of half again your height, in feet. If you're 6 feet tall, you can see 3 miles. From 600 feet up you can see 30 miles (the square root of 900). Conversely, you can see a 150-foot building from 15 miles away (the square root of 225).
Dani Zweig, Pittsburgh, Pennsylvania

513. SQUARE DANCING The fact that someone is a square or contra dancer greatly increases the chance that he or she is also a computer programmer or scientist (at least in Colorado, Vermont, and Washington). *Ellen Klaver, musician, Boulder, Colorado*

514. ORGANIZING PEOPLE A cooperative effort loses effectiveness when it includes more than fifteen people.
Peter Reimuller, Point Arena, California

515. PLANNING STAIRS A flight of stairs in a home should have thirteen risers. *Alex Fraser, Washington, D.C.*

516. WATCHING THE WIND Wind from the west, sailors like best. Wind from the north, sailors go forth. Wind from the east, sailors like least. Wind from the south, you shutta you mouth.
W. R. C. Shedenhelm, wind salesman, Encino, California

517. NOT WAITING TOO LONG Life will be easier if you go to bed before you get sleepy, eat before you get hungry, and clean your desk before you quit for the day.
V. G. Walkendifer, Churchton, Maryland

JON REIS

518. BUDGETING SOLDIERS   In ground warfare, one man behind a fortification is equal to five in the open field.
Scott Parker, Beaumont, Texas

519. NEEDING AN EDITOR   An author's willingness to allow his prose to be edited is inversely proportional to its need to be edited.   *Larry Kessenich, editor, Boston, Massachusetts*

520. TIMING A SCRIPT It takes 1½ to 2 minutes to perform an average page of script. A seventy-page script is about right for most plays.
Kelly Yeaton, teacher and stage manager, State College, Pennsylvania

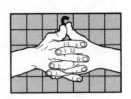

521. THE RULE OF CONTRARY INVESTING In the stock market, whatever the crowd does, do the opposite.
Lou Aleksich, Jr., Billings, Montana

522. LOSING WEIGHT The best way to lose weight is to leave food on the plate. *Mrs. Eileen Lightfoot, Burlington, Iowa*

523. THE CURIOUS RULE OF FARTS A farting horse will never tire; a farting man is one to hire.
From Walla Walla, Washington, circa 1940, via Louis G. Heibel, Alexandria, Virginia

524. WEIGHING WHALES To estimate the weight of a gray whale, figure one ton per foot of length.
Anonymous whale watcher, Marina del Rey, California

525. WEIGHING YOUR SKIN To estimate the weight of your skin, divide your weight by sixteen.
Scott M. Kruse, biogeographer, Fresno, California

526. SHOWING A DOG The more nervous you are while showing your dog, the more nervous your dog will be.
Kari Casher, breeder of Australian terriers, Oakland, California

527. INSPECTING SPECTACLES When trying on glasses, put them on and look at your feet. If they start to slip off your face, they are too loose.
Paul Lampe, writer and poet, St. Louis, Missouri

528. CHOOSING A CAR You'll get more money at resale time if you buy a red car. *Paul Lampe, writer and poet, St. Louis, Missouri*

529. KEEPING A CAR For every dollar of gas you put into your car each year, you'll need to put in a dollar's worth of repairs or maintenance. *Rev. Dan Orine, Athens, Georgia*

530. WATCHING YOUR COWS Expect a storm when your cows become agitated, start to bawl, and head for the barn.
Anonymous talk-show respondent, Burlington, Iowa

531. TRACKING A PAYROLL Every dollar of a paycheck turns over seven times in the local economy.
Scott Parker, Beaumont, Texas

It takes ten years
to recover from
serious use of LSD.

*Leonard Cohen, poet
and songwriter, quoted
in USA Today*

JON CRISPIN

532. MEASURING RICE   When using rice in casseroles or soups, use one handful per person.
J. Michaelson, asset manager, Phoenix, Arizona

533. SHOPPING A GARAGE SALE   If you want to save money at a garage sale, group a number of items together and offer a price for the group instead of bargaining for each item.
J. Michaelson, asset manager, Phoenix, Arizona

534. KNEADING BREAD   Knead bread dough until your arm is tired and then do twenty-five more punches.
J. Michaelson, asset manager, Phoenix, Arizona

535. TRACKING A DIABETIC   If you find ants around a toilet, suspect that a diabetic is using it.
Gerry M. Flick, M.D., ship's surgeon, S.S. Constitution

536. BUYING SHOES FOR KIDS   Four-year-olds will wear out the tops of their shoes before wearing out the soles, but they usually will outgrow them before either happens.
Denis Smith, school counselor, Camarillo, California

537. CATALOGING A LIBRARY   For a single-subject library — a medical library for example — use the Library of Congress cataloging system. For a general-interest library, use the Dewey decimal system.
Denis Smith, school counselor, Camarillo, California

538. SIZING A SKYLIGHT   For kitchens, porches, and bathrooms, a skylight that takes up 15 percent of the ceiling will provide good illumination. Family rooms and bedrooms need 10 percent, while hallways and attics need as little as 5 percent.
Scott Parker, Beaumont, Texas

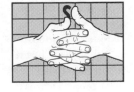

539. LEAVING A TIP   You should always leave at least twenty-five cents per plate for breakfast, fifty cents per plate for lunch, one dollar per plate for dinner, or 15 percent of the bill, whichever is higher.
Bernice Duda, grandmother and part-time waitress, Chicago, Illinois

540. BUYING JUST THE MATTRESS   If you want to buy just the mattress, take the price of a box spring and mattress set, divide by two, and add $25 to find out what you'll pay.
James Parker, civil engineer, Medford, Massachusetts

541. PLANTING A TREE   When you're planting a tree, make the hole twice as wide and twice as deep as the root ball. Then refill the hole one fourth of the way with good soil before putting in the tree.
Andrea Frankel, computer scientist, engineer, and holistic health practitioner, San Diego, California

542. ORDERING CHINESE   A Chinese restaurant that features Polynesian cocktails is unlikely to use authentic seasonings.   *Bruce Reznick, associate professor of mathematics, Urbana, Illinois*

543. RAISING THE RENT   A 1 percent increase in interest rates requires a 5 percent increase in rents.
Tony Gaenslen, amateur landlord, somewhere in New Hampshire

544. CHOOSING A HAT   Never wear a hat that has more character than you.
Bill Spivey, San Francisco, California, quoting Michael Harris, hat maker

545. PLAYING POKER   It is time to quit playing poker when you get so sleepy that you can't remember your hole card and you have to keep checking it.   *Bill Spivey, San Francisco, California*

546. POWERING YOUR BODY   Your body runs on about the same energy as a one hundred-watt bulb. About a quarter of the energy goes to your muscles, including your heart. Another quarter goes to the liver and spleen. Only about one fifth is consumed by the brain.   *Scott Parker, Beaumont, Texas*

547. CURBING SQUABBLES   If a supervisor spends more than 10 percent of her time dealing with the squabbles of subordinates, the organization is overstaffed and the subordinates do not have enough work.
Dirck Z. Meengs, management consultant, Canoga Park, California

JON CRISPIN

548. FINDING BOTTLES IN GEORGIA   Only one in ten bottles tossed on the roadside in Georgia will be returnable, and six of the remaining nine will be beer bottles.
Rusty Cartmill, student newspaper editor, University of Georgia

549. FINDING DIRTY MAGAZINES   Two out of every three magazines tossed along roadsides will be pornographic.
Rusty Cartmill, student newspaper editor, University of Georgia

550. THE NEW HAMPSHIRE RULE OF DROUGHT   If the ash buds before the oak, look for fire and smoke. If the oak buds before the ash, look for a summer splash!
Mr. and Mrs. Stearns Smalley, Wonalancet, New Hampshire

551. TESTING YOUR SEX DRIVE   Your sex drive is inversely proportional to the sensitivity of your funny bone.
Bob Cornett, photographer, New York City

552. SUFFERING A STROKE OR HEART ATTACK   You are most likely to suffer a stroke or heart attack between eight and nine in the morning.   *Scott Parker, Beaumont, Texas*

553. DRIVING ALONE AT NIGHT   When you're driving alone overnight, resist the temptation to rely on one long nap in the middle of the trip. Instead, take two short naps, with an hour of driving in between. This maximizes the amount of deep sleep per driving time.   *Phil A. Schrodt, associate professor, Northwestern University*

554. JOHN'S RULE OF FOREIGN TRAVEL   The softer the currency, the harder the toilet paper.
John Fountain, Riverside, Connecticut

555. TAPPING MAPLE TREES FOR SAP   To keep from girdling a maple tree when tapping it for sap, figure that an area the size of your hand dies around each tap and avoid that area in following years.   *Debby Hart, carpenter, Ithaca, New York*

556. SIZING-UP A BUSINESS   If the clerical staff is pleasant, you can bet that their bosses are pleasant to work for.
Gerald Gutlipp, mathematician, Chicago, Illinois

557. CHOOSING A SHOW FOR YOUR CRAFTS   Craft show attendance figures are exaggerated. Cut the advertised attendance figures in half and expect even less.
Bob Van Streader, Wood 'n Indian, Rochester, New York

558. KEEPING YOUR KIDS IN SHOES   Children aged six to ten outgrow their shoes every eighty-four days.
Mason Speed, WTKO radio, Ithaca, New York

559. EATING AN ELEPHANT   One elephant will provide as much meat as one hundred antelopes.
Pygmy hunters in the Ituri Forest of Zaire, from "Nova" on PBS

560. BREATHING THROUGH YOUR HEATER COIL   Check your car's heater coil for obstructions after you back-flush it. If you can blow through it as easily as you can breathe, it's free of debris.   *Steve Overback, radio announcer*

561. THE HISTORIC RULE OF VAUDEVILLE   A vaudeville act with a harp always got $5 more than one without a harp.
Minnie Marx, mother of Harpo Marx, cited by Bill Marx, Harpo's son

562. CUTTING A DIAMOND   A cut and polished diamond will weigh half what it did in the rough.   *Darryl T. Mix, Phoenix, Arizona*

563. LIMING A LAKE   It takes about 2½ tons of limestone per acre of lake to neutralize the effects of acid rain.
K. Hammond, Wilmington, Delaware

564. HOLDING AN ODD INVESTMENT   You should be willing to hold an odd investment like stamps or coins for three to five years.
Michael Weinstein, The Gold and Silver Galleries, Ithaca, New York

565. DESIGNING AN AD   If an ad is well designed, it will look just as good upside down.
Michele Rogers, advertising creative director, Warwick, Rhode Island

566. MOWING A WET LAWN   The lawn is too wet to mow until all the puddles evaporate from the asphalt driveway.
Brad Edmondson, writer, Ithaca, New York

When a matchmaking friend describes a potential date as "sweet, friendly, and intelligent," you can be sure he or she won't be much to look at. This is true even when you are hoping it might be an exception.

Johnnie Putnam, WIND radio, Chicago, Illinois

JON CRISPIN

567. CHOOSING A DIET   A prudent diet is one in which less than 35 percent of your calories come from fat.
Kenneth Jackson, dietician, New York City

568. LOSING AN ARGUMENT IN JAPAN   In Japan, the first person to raise his voice loses the argument.
Cally Arthur, managing editor, Alpine, New York

569. UNDERSTANDING SOMEONE   If you're trying to understand what a person is thinking or feeling, mirror that person's behavior. Look at what they are looking at and mimic their body language.
Kelly Yeaton, teacher and stage manager, State College, Pennsylvania

570. CHOOSING A MARGARINE   Regarding cholesterol content, the margarine sold in tubs is better for you than that sold in sticks.
Dr. Stephen S. Scheidt, professor of clinical medicine, Cornell University Medical College, New York City

571. LOWERING YOUR BLOOD CHOLESTEROL   For every 1 percent drop in your blood cholesterol, you get a 2 percent drop in your risk of a heart attack.
Dr. Stephen S. Scheidt, professor of clinical medicine, Cornell University Medical College, New York City

572. CHECKING FOR SUNBURN   You can check if you're starting to get a sunburn by pressing an exposed part of your body with your finger. If the skin you pressed is white when you lift your finger, you're beginning to burn.
Elsbeth Cates, writer, Rising Star, North Dakota, in New Age Journal

573. CHECKING FOR STRESS   Under normal temperature conditions, warm hands indicate relaxation, cool hands indicate tension. Place your hands on your neck, which is always warm; if they feel cool, concentrate on relaxing.   *Jan Lowenstein, writer*

574. USING A REFRIGERATOR-FREEZER   Don't even consider freezing a large amount of food in the freezer compartment of a conventional refrigerator. Add no more than three pounds of unfrozen food for each cubic foot of space in the box.
The Lobel brothers, butcher shop owners, New York City

575. PLANTING YOUR PEAS   When you see coots in the pond in the park, you know it's warm enough to plant peas.
Peggy Macneale, writer, Flower and Garden

576. PLANNING A WEDDING   You need two ushers for every fifty wedding guests.   *Rose Rollins, Greenville, South Carolina*

577. SAVING LIVES IN NEW YORK   Every 1 percent increase in seat belt use prevents eight deaths and 360 serious injuries per year in New York State.
The Governor's Traffic Safety Committee, New York State

578. PLANNING A TELEVISION AD   The visual part of a TV commercial accounts for 85 percent of the impact on the viewer; the sound track accounts for 15 percent.
John Koten, staff reporter, Wall Street Journal

579. EATING LIKE A THIN PERSON   Before you eat, ask yourself how hungry you are on a scale from 1 to 10 — 1 representing a growling stomach and 10 representing the stuffed, bloated, I-think-I'm-going-to-die feeling often experienced after Thanksgiving dinner. Eat only when you rate your hunger a 1 or 2. Then stop when you reach 5.
Evette M. Hackman, R.D., Ph.D., consulting nutritionist, BHIHRI

580. MAKING A NAME IN MATHEMATICS   In the field of mathematics, if you haven't made an important discovery by the time you're twenty-two, you probably never will.
Gerald Gutlipp, mathematician, Chicago, Illinois

581. DESIGNING AN ELEVATOR   Traveling faster than ten miles per hour in an elevator will make your ears pop.
Scott Parker, Beaumont, Texas

582. FOLLOWING INTEREST RATES   On a fifteen-year adjustable-rate mortgage, every percentage-point rise in interest will boost your monthly payment by about 5 percent.
William C. Banks, writer, Money

JON REIS

583. CHOOSING A FIN FOR A SAILBOARD The higher the
wind, the smaller the fin.
Jeremy Bishop, windsurfing shop owner, Myers Point, New York

584. SWITCHING TO A SHORTER SAILBOARD If the least
experienced windsurfers are getting catapulted over their sails,
then it's time to sail your shortboard.
Jeremy Bishop, windsurfing shop owner, Myers Point, New York

585. COUNTING WHITE CAPS   If there are more white caps than you can count, the wind is probably blowing over fifteen knots.   *Jeremy Bishop, windsurfing shop owner, Myers Point, New York*

586. THE WINDSURFING RULE OF 35/35   In a 35-knot wind, you need a 35-square foot sail for windsurfing. For every 5 knots of wind less, add 5 square feet of sail. For flat water, add an extra 5 square feet.
Jeremy Bishop, windsurfing shop owner, Myers Point, New York

587. CHOOSING A SAILBOARD   Beginning windsurfers should use a sailboard that is from 20 to 40 liters of volume greater than their body weight. A 150-pound person should sail a board that has 170 to 190 liters of volume.
Jeremy Bishop, windsurfing shop owner, Myers Point, New York

588. UPHAULING A SHORTBOARD   You can uphaul a sail-board that is up to thirty liters less than your body weight in pounds.   *Jeremy Bishop, windsurfing shop owner, Myers Point, New York*

589. MEASURING THE PROGRESS OF A PREGNANCY
Lay a cloth tape measure over the belly, pressing one end on the pubic bone. The number of centimeters from the pubic bone to the top of the uterus is the number of weeks of pregnancy.
John McPhee in The New Yorker, *quoting Dr. Ann Dorney*

590. ESTIMATING TIME OF DEATH   To estimate the length of time a person has been dead, take a rectal temperature. If it is above room temperature, subtract from ninety-eight. The answer is the number of hours since death.
Thomas O. Marsh, writer and coroner's investigator, Fairfield, Ohio

591. DETERMINING THE HEALTH OF A FARM   If a farm has a debt-to-asset ratio of more than 70 percent, it is in severe trouble. If the debt-to-asset ratio is between 40 and 70 percent, the farm is facing serious problems. And if the debt-to-asset ratio is less than 30 percent, the operator is safe.
Rex R. Campbell, professor of rural sociology, University of Missouri, in American Demographics

592. SHOPPING LIQUIDATION SALES   Items at liquidation sales should sell for about one-tenth their regular price.
J. Michael Kanouff, writer, Home Mechanix

593. INVESTING IN TIMBER   To be a worthwhile investment, a timberland should be at least three hundred acres, be accessible by a paved road, and have good soil.
George Baker, manager of Merrill Lynch's timber division, in the Wall Street Journal

This book contains rules of thumb from every state except Idaho, Utah, and Wyoming. I'd like to know what's going on out there. Don't get me wrong. I'm not saying it's anything strange, but I looked at a map, and Idaho, Utah, and Wyoming are about the same size as that place off Bermuda where all the airplanes disappear. They form kind of a triangle too. Well, I'm not into that conspiracy stuff, I'm just saying it's funny that there are no rules of thumb from Idaho, Utah, and Wyoming. O.K., maybe it's a coincidence, but they do say the West has its mysteries. All I know is that as far as rules of thumb go, it's quiet out there. Too quiet.

594. AVOIDING SHIPS AT SEA   To avoid being run down by other ships on the ocean, check the horizon every fifteen minutes. A fast ship can get dangerously close within fifteen minutes. *Rick Eckstrom, builder, Danby, New York*

595. WRITING SENTENCES   Professional writers average about twenty words per sentence.   *Scott Parker, Beaumont, Texas*

596. FINDING YOUR DOMINANT EYE   To find your dominant eye, make a circle of your thumb and forefinger about six inches in front of your face. Look through the circle with both eyes at an object across the room. Now close one eye; if the object stays in the circle, the open eye is the dominant one. *Donald H. Dunn, in Business Week*

597. ESTIMATING THE WIND SPEED ABOVE   The wind velocity at two thousand feet is usually two to three times the speed at ground level.   *Richard L. Collins, editor in chief, Flying*

598. STAYING PROFICIENT AS A PILOT   You should fly at least one hundred hours a year to stay proficient as a fair-weather pilot. If you're flying on instruments, make that two hundred hours a year.   *Jack Barclay, biologist and flight instructor, Groton, New York*

599. AIMING A BALLISTIC MISSILE   Submarine-launched ballistic missiles lack the accuracy of ground-launched weapons. At best, you can expect one to land within fifteen hundred feet of a target.   *Drew Middleton, military analyst, New York Times*

600. THE HARLEY-DAVIDSON RULE   When in doubt, bore it out.   *Hunter S. Thompson, The Curse of Lono*

601. WATCHING YOUR DRINKING   You may be on the brink of a drinking problem if you're downing four alcoholic drinks a day, three times a week.   *J. R. Malone, Fairbanks, Alaska*

602. THE TEMPERATURE RULE   If you add eighteen degrees to the temperature at six A.M., you'll find the high temperature for the day. *John Schaedler, Schaedler Quinzel Lehnert Green, Inc., New York City*

603. USING A WORD PROCESSOR   Using a word processor will not save time; it will only increase quality. The time you save in retyping is canceled out by the time you spend making tiny revisions.   *Phil A. Schrodt, associate professor, Northwestern University*

604. SUPPORTING A CHILD   Child support payments for one child will usually equal 20 percent of the gross income of the parent who doesn't have custody.   *Carol Benjamin, Scottsdale, Arizona*

605. CHECKING YOUR WEIGHT   A man who is five feet tall should weigh 106 pounds. If taller, add six pounds for every inch of height. For example, a man who's five feet ten inches tall should weigh 166 pounds. A woman who's five feet tall should weigh 105 pounds. If taller, add five pounds for every inch of height.
Dr. Richard Freeman, vice chairman, Department of Medicine, University of Wisconsin, in USA Today

606. STARTING SWEET POTATOES   Sweet potatoes are started from slips, or cuttings. Eight potatoes will provide enough slips for a one-hundred-foot row of potatoes.
Gary Nelson, home gardener, Oakland, Arkansas, in Flower and Garden

607. DIPPING A BRUSH   Don't dip your paintbrush into the paint more than one-third to one-half the length of its exposed bristles.   *Joseph R. Provey, editor, Home Mechanix*

608. CHOOSING A WIG   A long face needs a full wig; a round face needs height at the crown, but a woman with an oval face can wear anything.
Eva Gabor, Eva Gabor International, the world's largest wig company

609. SPEEDING ON THE FREEWAY   If you must speed on a freeway, speed in the slow lane. Your chances of getting a ticket are one-fourth that of speeding in the fast lane.
Vince Mooney, real estate broker, Tulsa, Oklahoma

610. LISTENING TO PEEPERS   When the spring peepers start, the maple sugaring stops.
Cheryl Russell, demographer, editor in chief, American Demographics

611. PRUNING TREES   When pruning a branch from a tree, never leave a stub long enough to hang your hat on.
Ronald Newberry, retired, Cayutaville, New York

612. DEALING WITH A COMPUTER   When dealing with a computer, a good rule to remember is to treat it as you would a small retarded (but very obedient) child.
Bob Horton, consultant and writer, St. Petersburg, Florida

613. FOLLOWING UNEMPLOYMENT   For each 1 percent rise in unemployment, suicides increase by 4.1 percent and admissions to mental hospitals increase by 4.3 percent.
Scott Parker, Beaumont, Texas

614. THE SEVENTEENTH-CENTURY RULE   The best oil is on the top; the best wine is in the middle; and the best honey is on the bottom.   *Tom Robinson, computer programmer, Berkeley, California*

If a car that was working stops or won't start, the problem probably is simple to fix. Catastrophic failures of major parts are rare. The apparent frequency of major breakdowns is due to unscrupulous or lazy repair shops that don't look for the simple solutions and the publicity surrounding auto racing, where catastrophic failure is more common.

Phil A. Schrodt, associate professor, Northwestern University

615. COOLING WITH TREES   One large tree has the cooling power of five average-size air conditioners running twenty hours a day.   *Debra Prybyla, writer, The New York State Conservationist*

616. CHOOSING A BORDEAUX   Presidential-election-year Bordeaux are generally bad.
Mark Matthews, quoting Richard M. Nixon in The Washington Journalism Review

617. ACCEPTING A CHECK   Be wary when accepting a check with a check number lower than 250.
Sue Viders, The Artist's Magazine

618. WATCHING AMERICANS   Americans stand just far enough apart when talking that, with arms extended, they can insert their thumbs into each other's ears.
Roger Axtell, Janesville, Wisconsin, author of "Do's and Taboos Around the World," in The New Yorker

619. MARKETING TO THE ELDERLY   Elderly consumers think they are fifteen years younger than they actually are.
Tracy Lux Frances, Bradenton, Florida

620. ADJUSTING TO TIME ZONES   It takes your body one day to adjust for each time zone you cross. If you travel across three time zones, plan on spending three days adjusting to it.
Cheryl Russell, demographer, editor in chief, American Demographics

621. DESIGNING A MODERN CHAIR If you're designing a modern chair and want to know how well your design will stand the test of time, imagine thirty of them lined up in a laundromat. *Steve Carver, illustrator, Ithaca, New York*

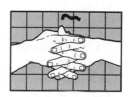

622. REDUCING YOUR SAMPLING ERROR Sampling error is an important factor in the interpretation of television audience ratings. To cut the sampling error by half, quadruple your sample size.
Hugh Malcolm Beville, Jr., author of Audience Ratings: Radio, Television, Cable

623. THROWING OUT CLOTHING Sometimes when cleaning out your closet you'll come across a garment that you don't wear much because no other clothes go with it. If you aren't ready to spend any money to make the item work for you, you probably are ready to give it to Goodwill. *Dalma Heyn, McCall's*

624. CHECKING THE PLUG If you have a computer problem and a knowledgeable person recommends that you check to see whether your computer is plugged in or all the cables are connected, check carefully, and don't be insulted — the symptoms aren't ambiguous. *Paul Hoffman, writer, Berkeley, California*

625. BUYING A NEW COMPUTER If you are unsure of yourself when buying a new computer, ask the same questions you would ask a new-car salesperson.
Paul Hoffman, writer, Berkeley, California

626. ESTIMATING THE VOLUME OF A TANK A cylindrical tank fifteen inches in diameter holds about one gallon for each inch of height. A thirty-inch-diameter tank holds four gallons per inch. *Millard Zeisberg, Elkton, Maryland*

627. THE SILICON VALLEY RULE To be considered a success in Silicon Valley, you must make more than twice your age in thousands of dollars, and your spouse must be less than half your age plus seven years. *Roy A. Berg, Los Altos, California*

628. THE NERD RULE A nerd never knows he's a nerd.
Paul Carter, ex-nerd, New York City

629. GETTING SICK ON A LUXURY SHIP The more expensive your cabin on a cruise, the greater the possibility that you will get seasick. On most luxury ships the expensive cabins are found forward, high above the waterline, and with outside bulkhead exposure. This subjects them to more rolling and pitching than the less expensive cabins located nearer the waterline, inside, and closer to the ship's center of gravity.
Gerry M. Flick, M.D., ship's surgeon, S.S. Constitution

When you're relaxed, twelve breaths is approximately equal to one minute.

Emmon Bodfish, Oakland, California

630. BUYING A NEW CAR   The best time to buy a new car is the last day of the month, because the sales staff want their monthly reports to look good and are more likely to bargain. You can increase your chances of getting a good deal by choosing the youngest salesperson on the floor.   *Scott Parker, Beaumont, Texas*

631. THE ILLUSTRATOR'S RULE   A free-lance illustrator needs to bill clients for three times the hourly rate he or she would like to earn at the drawing board. The extra will just cover overhead, hustling, daydreaming, and other non-billables. *Jon Buller, Lyme, Connecticut*

632. PROTECTING YOUR DATA   In the computer world, make a copy of anything that's important. If it's really important, make two copies.   *Tom Meritt, computer systems specialist*

633. SHOOTING PHOTOGRAPHS   A professional photographer should plan on exposing one roll of film per hour on the job.   *Jon Reis, photographer, Ithaca, New York*

634. RUNNING A PHOTOGRAPHY STUDIO   For every hour photographers are on the job shooting film, they spend four hours working in the studio.   *Jon Reis, photographer, Ithaca, New York*

635. FOLLOWING CORRUPTION   The amount of corruption in a society is directly proportional to the number of laws that the society has.   *Jim Butler, Keala Kekua, Hawaii*

636. MAKING TIME IN A KAYAK   In moderate white water, expect to average about four to five miles per hour if you paddle straight downriver and don't stop to play.
Martha Betcher, medical technician, Incline Village, Nevada

637. LEANING A KAYAK   In a kayak, remember to lean downstream.   *Martha Betcher, medical technician, Incline Village, Nevada*

638. FINDING DEEP WATER   To find the deepest water in a river, look for the middle of the inverted V of glossy water where the main current flows. At a bend in a river, the water is deepest on the outside of the turn.
Martha Betcher, medical technician, Incline Village, Nevada

639. SERVING POTATOES AND ROLLS   For the average dinner, plan on one medium potato per person and 1½ dinner rolls.
Myrtle F. Synquist, Burlington, Iowa

640. PAINTING YOUR DINING ROOM   If you paint your dining room peach, your mealtimes will be more harmonious.
Diana Souza, illustrator, Ithaca, New York

641. BUYING CLOTHES   If you have to convince yourself that you want a particular article of clothing, don't buy it — you'll be adding another dust collector to your closet.
Andrea Frankel, computer scientist, engineer, and holistic health practitioner, San Diego, California

642. MEASURING SOCIAL STABILITY   To measure the social stability of a country, compare the income of the top tenth of the population with that of the bottom tenth. If the top tenth is getting more than fifteen times the income of the bottom tenth, you've got a problem.
Daniel Shively, Indiana, Pennsylvania, quoting futurist Marvin Cetron

643. KEEPING YOURSELF IN SHOES   If you switch back and forth among three pairs of shoes, they will last as long as five pairs worn out one pair at a time.
Joe Cosentini, shoe store owner, Ithaca, New York

644. BUYING A HAND TOOL   Never buy a hand tool that does not have the manufacturer's name permanently inscribed on it. The absence of a name indicates poor quality.
Dirck Z. Meengs, management consultant, Canoga Park, California

645. SIZING-UP A CALLER   Usually a telephone caller makes three points. The third one is the real reason for the call.
Peter A. Lake, Marina del Rey, California

JON REIS

646. CALLY'S COFFEE RULE   It takes four hours to go to sleep after your last cup of coffee.
Cally Arthur, managing editor, Alpine, New York

647. WATCHING WIDOWS   You know a widow has recovered from the death of her husband when she starts reading <u>Gourmet</u> again.   *Robin Masson, attorney and law professor, Ithaca, New York*

648. GIVING AWAY MONEY   You are rich enough to give small amounts of money to worthy causes when you can buy all the groceries you need.   *Sharon K. Yntema, writer, Ithaca, New York*

649. THE PAPER MONEY RULE   You are close to poverty when paper towels are a luxury item.
Sharon K. Yntema, writer, Ithaca, New York

650. PICKING A NEW PLACE TO LIVE   You can live happily in a new house or apartment if, on your first visit, you immediately can visualize yourself and your family engaged in your usual activities among your current possessions. If you have to stop and think about how you'd use each area or how your furniture would fit in the place, forget it.
Andrea Frankel, computer scientist, engineer, and holistic health practitioner, San Diego, California

651. RUBENKING'S PARADOXICAL RULE   Writing the first 90 percent of a computer program takes 90 percent of the time. The remaining 10 percent also takes 90 percent of the time, and the final touches also take 90 percent of the time.
Neil J. Rubenking, microcomputer consultant, San Francisco, California

652. WATCHING HORSES YAWN When a horse yawns, the weather's going to change. *Rita Pitkin, Albany, Vermont*

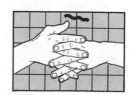

653. CHOOSING FLOOR JOISTS When you are building a floor, use joists hefty enough to limit deflection at the center of the floor to ⅟₃₆₀th of the span.
Albert G. H. Dietz, Dwelling House Construction

654. PARKING AT CHURCH A church needs two acres of parking for every three hundred members.
Mary Ellen Parker, teacher, Cincinnati, Ohio

655. UNDERSTANDING FRENCH French speakers use twice as many syllables per sentence as English speakers. That's why French is so hard to understand. *Sid Ore, Paris, France*

656. MANAGING YOUR WEIGHT Your weight should vary to the extent that your wardrobe can handle it.
sunny bat-or, star of "Fit, Fat, and Fabulous," Ithaca, New York

657. PLANTING PEAS IN MASSACHUSETTS In Massachusetts, plant your peas by Patriot's Day and harvest them by the Fourth of July. *Sid Ore, Paris, France*

658. PACKING UP A ROCK BAND If you are in a four-piece rock band, it takes about eight hours to pack up your equipment, travel to your local gig, unload, set up, play one set, break down, load up, and return home. Add one-half hour for each additional piece, and add one hour for each additional set played.
Mark McMullen, accountant, Alexandria, Virginia

659. LOCATING A STUD If you need to locate a stud in a stick-framed wall, remember that most electricians are right-handed. Find an outlet, and tap the wall directly to its left. The odds are in your favor that the stud will be there, and you can measure away from it in sixteen-inch increments to find other studs. *Art McAfee, Edmonton, Alberta, in Fine Homebuilding*

660. CARRYING EXTRA WEIGHT Carrying a one-pound weight in each hand while walking boosts your energy expenditure by about 1 percent. Carrying the same weights on your feet boosts your energy expenditure by about 2 percent.
Ned Frederick, writer, Exeter, New Hampshire

661. GROWING ONIONS The smaller the onion sets, the larger the onions. *Paul Bauer, West Harrison, Indiana*

It's not that easy to come up with a rule of thumb out of the blue. Sometimes it helps to start with a problem. Here's a rule of thumb I'd like to have: How do you tell if someone is tall or short when you only have a picture of his head? There must be someone clever enough to develop a rule of thumb to separate tall people from short people by looking at a photo of their face.

662. CHOOSING A SPOUSE If your fiancé does something that bothers you before you're married, it will bother you ten times more after you're married.
Bruno Colapietro, matrimonial lawyer with over eight thousand cases, Binghamton, New York

663. ORDERING CHINESE When you order Chinese food, order one entrée less than the number of people in the group to avoid unwanted leftovers. *Claire Forchheimer, Flushing, New York*

664. GETTING STARTED WITH CATTLE When starting out, raise the same breed of cattle as your neighbors. Specialize later, when you have experience.
Ken Scharabok, financial manager, Dayton, Ohio

665. BUYING FENCE FOR CATTLE Regular cattle fencing costs $2,500 to $3,000 per mile. Electric fencing costs about $100 per mile. *Ken Scharabok, financial manager, Dayton, Ohio*

666. CONVERTING APARTMENTS TO CONDOMINIUMS When converting apartments to condominiums, you must be able to sell all the condos for a total of twice the price you paid for the apartment building or you won't make any money.
Vince Mooney, real estate broker, Tulsa, Oklahoma

667. MANAGING AN APARTMENT For unfurnished apartments, expect a tenant turnover of about 45 percent per year.
Scott Parker, Beaumont, Texas

668. MEASURING INTELLIGENCE WITH BUTTONS Intelligence can be measured by the number of buttons fastened on a person's shirt. The more buttons fastened, the higher the IQ.
Curtis Cloaninger, agriculture teacher, Asheville, North Carolina

669. LOOKING GOOD ON TV #1 You always look 15 percent more serious on TV than you do in real life, so try to look 15 percent less serious when you are on camera.
Sharon K. Yntema, writer, Ithaca, New York

670. LOOKING GOOD ON TV #2 You will look alert on TV if you lean forward. You will look even more alert if you cross your legs. *Sharon K. Yntema, writer, Ithaca, New York*

671. FIXING YOUR FACE FOR TV For TV appearances, match the color of your make-up to the color of the tip of your tongue. *Sharon K. Yntema, writer, Ithaca, New York*

672. DEALING WITH RUDE DRIVERS The harder you have to brake to avoid hitting someone who pulls in front of you, the sooner you'll have to brake for him when he turns off.
Tania Werbizky, historic preservationist, Ithaca, New York

673. FINISHING WOOD   If there's any question about when to do some finish work on a woodworking project, do it immediately. Chances are you won't do it later.
Phil Tomlinson, builder, Ithaca, New York

674. CREATING PROBLEMS   A creative person is thirty-five times more likely than the average person to need treatment for a mental problem.   *Scott Parker, Beaumont, Texas, quoting* Omni

675. TASTING A CHAMPAGNE   A yeasty taste means a young champagne that could use more time in the bottle.
Rick Eckstrom, builder and wine maker, Danby, New York

676. FINISHING A SOFTWARE PROJECT   Adding manpower to a late software project will, more times than not, make it even later.
Joan Howe, Arlington, Massachusetts, quoting Frederick P. Brooks, Jr., The Mythical Man-Month

677. BUDGETING YOUR SOFTWARE PROJECT TIME
When you budget your time for a software job, figure one third for planning, one sixth for coding, one fourth for component and early system tests, and one fourth for final system tests.
Joan Howe, Arlington, Massachusetts, quoting Frederick P. Brooks, Jr., The Mythical Man-Month

678. SPOTTING AN UNDERCOVER DETECTIVE   A person who walks with only one arm swinging is likely to be a cop.
B. Wiggins, artist, New York City

679. WATCHING FOR COPS   If a car following you at night doesn't have perfectly aligned headlights, it is not a police car.
Eric Kimple, motorcycle racer, Columbus, Ohio

680. DEALING WITH LAUNDRY   An average adult will generate one load of dirty laundry per week. Athletes, children, and people who work outdoors will generate twice that much.
Gail Smith, parts unknown

681. INCREASING YOUR PERFORMANCE   Up to a limit of ten hours, every hour you add to your weekly fitness training can increase your athletic performance by 5 percent.
Ned Frederick, writer, Exeter, New Hampshire

682. COOKING A STEAK   If you want a medium-rare steak, it should be as firm as the puffy area between your thumb and index finger. If you want your steak rarer, it should be softer; more done, harder.
J. Harb, sous-chef, Restaurant La Résidence, Chapel Hill, North Carolina

A good speech will present one idea per five-minute period, but no more than two or three ideas in a twenty-minute talk.

Roberta Prescott, writer, USAir

JON CRISPIN

683. MAKING BEER   You need six pounds of sugar to make five gallons of home-brewed beer.
Tom Robinson, computer programmer, Berkeley, California

684. STORING BEER   You lose one day of shelf life for every degree you let your beer get above 20° C.
Dave Graham, engineer and authority on beer

685. USING A SUPERCOMPUTER   A supercomputer operating at the highest frontier speeds will fail every month or so.
Kevin Kelly, quoting Seymour Cray, computer wizard

686. TAKING A LIE DETECTOR TEST   If you are innocent, do not take a lie detector test. If you're guilty, take it, because it may exonerate you.   *Kevin Kelly, quoting Discover*

687. CHECKING YOUR STOOL   A healthy bowel movement should be the consistency of soft-serve ice cream and should float. Sinkers indicate inadequate fiber in the diet.
Cindy Watanabe, Honolulu, Hawaii

688. EDITING SLIDES FOR A PRESENTATION   When you're choosing slides for a presentation, spread them on a light table and toss out any that have type too small to read with the unaided eye.   *Tim McGrath, engineer, Boston, Massachusetts*

689. MANAGING PARKING METERS   Most cities can expect the annual income from parking meter fines to be twice the income from parking meter deposits.
Marie E. Witmer, director of technical services, Institutional and Municipal Parking Congress, Fredricksburg, Virginia

690. MEASURING CRICKETS   A quart jar will hold one thousand crickets.
Jack Armstrong, president, American Cricket Growers Association, West Monroe, Louisiana

691. FOLLOWING LABOR #1   If a woman can talk on the telephone during a contraction, the birth is a long way off. If the woman can't speak during a contraction, birth is near.
Dr. K. Emmott, Vancouver, British Columbia

692. FOLLOWING LABOR #2   If a woman can walk around during contractions, she is not fully dilated.
Dr. K. Emmott, Vancouver, British Columbia

693. FOLLOWING LABOR #3   If the waters do not break at the start of the labor, they will break at the start of the pushing stage.   *Dr. K. Emmott, Vancouver, British Columbia*

694. FOLLOWING LABOR #4   If a husband calls saying his wife (pregnant with their first child) is having really strong contractions, the birth is a long way off, but tell them to come to the hospital anyway.   *Dr. K. Emmott, Vancouver, British Columbia*

695. FOLLOWING LABOR #5   If a woman is in labor and you want to know if there is time to get her to the hospital, check for the child's head during a contraction. If you can't see it and it is the woman's first child, you have at least an hour. If you can see a quarter's worth, you have twenty or thirty minutes. If you can see a quarter's worth and she has had a child before, you don't have time.   *Dr. K. Emmott, Vancouver, British Columbia*

696. EDITING A NEWSPAPER   Kill everything that you don't understand.   *Joel Garreau, editor, Washington Post*

697. WATCHING BIRDS   If you see birds rotating way up — turning small, tight circles and not flapping their wings — you're going to get a blow.
Alec Wilkinson, The New Yorker, quoting Raymond Duarte, Provincetown, Massachusetts

698. THE HEART RULE   A healthy person's heart is about the size of his or her fist.
Thomas O. Marsh, writer and coroner's investigator, Fairfield, Ohio

699. USING PHOTOGRAPHIC FILTERS   Any filter will lighten objects of its own color and darken those of a complementary hue.   *Paul Lisseck, flower photographer, Ithaca, New York*

> Do not start a new business unless you can wait at least one year before realizing a profit.
>
> *Thomas O. Marsh, writer, Fairfield, Ohio*

700. HAULING BOOKS   You can fit two thousand mass market paperbacks in a Datsun pickup.
Dave Ewan, Wind Chimes Book Exchange, Millville, New Jersey

701. STOCKING A BOOKSTORE #1   A bookstore needs to stock a minimum of ten thousand titles to have any hope of having what people ask for.
Dave Ewan, Wind Chimes Book Exchange, Millville, New Jersey

702. STOCKING A BOOKSTORE #2 If you stock six of any bookstore item, you'll sell three in one week, two more in one month, and still have the last one when you retire.
Dave Ewan, Wind Chimes Book Exchange, Millville, New Jersey

703. SELLING BOOKS Ten percent of bookstore customers buy 90 percent of the books. Ten percent never buy anything.
Dave Ewan, Wind Chimes Book Exchange, Millville, New Jersey

704. LIGHTING A BOOKSTORE One continuous strip of fluorescent lights eight feet high along the center of each aisle is enough light for a bookstore.
Dave Ewan, Wind Chimes Book Exchange, Millville, New Jersey

705. REPORTING A DEMONSTRATION The police will report that only one-third to one-half as many people were at a demonstration as were actually there. Newspapers will do the same. Television will reduce the number even more.
Ellen Klaver, musician, Boulder, Colorado

706. OFFERING HELP Some people aren't really looking for help. If someone responds to three valid suggestions with a "yes, but . . . ," he or she is more interested in playing games than solving problems.
Andrea Frankel, computer scientist, engineer, and holistic health practitioner, San Diego, California

707. PREPARING FROZEN FOODS When cooking a frozen meal, always increase the maximum recommended cooking time by 10 to 15 percent. When warming a frozen pizza, add oregano. With all other foods, add butter.
Markus Mueller, student, Pepper Pike, Ohio

708. FINDING TORNADOS Most tornados are found in the vicinity of mobile homes, and vice versa.
Framine Green, Cherry Hill, New Jersey

709. MAKING GARBAGE The average person generates one ton of garbage per year.
Ellen Marsh, conference manager, King Ferry, New York

710. TIPPING THE PORTER Tip the porter a buck a bag.
Jon Reis, photographer, Ithaca, New York

711. BEATING A RAP If a patrolman pulls you over and gets out of his car, get out of your car and meet him. This puts you on a person-to-person rather than a cop-to-driver footing, and it may lead to a warning instead of a ticket.
Ashley Day Leavitt, Dover, New Jersey

No more than 10 percent of the people in an apartment complex will try to use the pool at the same time, and about 80 percent will never use it.

Vince Mooney, real estate broker, Tulsa, Oklahoma

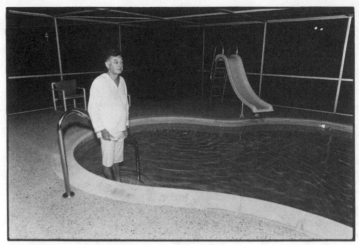

712. SELLING YOUR PHOTOGRAPHS   Photographs on file with a stock agency will bring you fifty cents per image per year.   *Jon Reis, photographer, Ithaca, New York*

713. CATCHING A PYROMANIAC   A pyromaniac is proud of his work, and may be found in the crowd watching the fire. A professional arsonist will be somewhere else, establishing an alibi.   *Anonymous*

714. ED'S RULE OF HUNTING DUCKS   Wind in the east, ducks fly the least.   *Ed Timmerman, duck hunter, Burlington, Iowa*

715. WATCHING YOUR HEART WHEN YOU WAKE   Keep tabs on your heartbeat at rest first thing in the morning. An increase of seven beats or more per minute is a sign of overtraining.
Ned Frederick, writer, quoting track coach Dick Brown, Exeter, New Hampshire

716. ANTICIPATING GALL BLADDER PROBLEMS   White women with blond hair, light skin, and light eyes are the most likely victims of gall bladder problems.   *Scott Parker, Beaumont, Texas*

717. HUNTING A JOB   In your first interview, don't ask about vacations, pay, pensions, or working hours. Doing so will give the impression you are looking for an easy job. First get an offer, then tell the employer what you want.
John Munschauer, author of Jobs for English Majors and Other Smart People

718. PLANNING INTERVIEWS   Interview first for the jobs you care about least. The experience will improve your important interviews.
John Munschauer, author of Jobs for English Majors and Other Smart People

719. USING SEMICOLONS   When in doubt, use the semicolon; the average reader won't understand its use and will give you credit for erudition.
Denis Smith, school counselor, Camarillo, California

720. LARRY COOPER'S RULE   Most semicolons are unnecessary. If God wanted us to use them, he would have put one next to our large intestines.
Larry Cooper, manuscript editor, Swampscott, Massachusetts

721. CHECKING YOUR BAGGAGE   If you have more than ten bags, immediately tip the porter $20. More times than not, he will check your luggage through without excess-baggage charges.
David Gluck, cinematographer, Photosynthesis Productions, Ithaca, New York

722. DOING THERAPY WITH FRIENDS   Let your friend be a client and you'll end up with neither.
Jeffrey A. Schaler, gestalt therapist, Silver Spring, Maryland

723. CARRYING CLOUT   In any group, the person doing the least talking is the one with the most power.
David Lyon, writer and advertising authority, Westport, Connecticut

724. SELLING AND TALKING   The sale is made while the customer is talking.
David Lyon, writer and advertising authority, Westport, Connecticut

725. RUNNING ADS ON TV   You should run a TV commercial at least four times a day, four days a week, three weeks a month. If you run it less than that, your ad money would be better spent elsewhere.   *Scott Parker, Beaumont, Texas*

726. THE MILITARY RULE   If it moves, salute it. If it don't, paint it.
Ronald R. Hodge, investment executive and commercial pilot, Long Beach, California

727. MAILING YOUR FILM   You can send 110 and 126 cartridge film through the mail using only one twenty-two-cent stamp without incurring postage due, although nearly all developers recommend using two stamps.
Rusty Cartmill, student newspaper editor, University of Georgia

728. WARMING UP YOUR CAR   The time it takes to clean off the windshield is the time it takes to warm up your engine.
Robert A. Shapiro, charter pilot, Ithaca, New York

729. BOB'S RULE FOR DOUBLING YOUR MONEY The quickest way to double your money is to fold it over once and put it back in your pocket. *Bob Larson, Stuttgart, Germany*

730. WATCHING PISTOLS IN PLAYS If there is a pistol on the wall in the first act, it will be fired by the third act. *Bob Larson, Stuttgart, Germany, quoting Anton Chekhov*

731. PERUSING A NURSING HOME If you smell urine when you enter a nursing home, it is not a place to put someone you care about. *Edward J. Garrison, nursing home administrator, Watsonville, California*

732. CHECKING A REFERENCE If you are checking a reference and you ask someone's former employer, "Would you hire this person again?" any answer but "yes" is a "no." *Edward J. Garrison, nursing home administrator, Watsonville, California*

733. PREHEATING AN OVEN Ovens are always preheated to 350 degrees. No more, no less. *Gordon Hard, assistant editor, Consumer Reports*

734. COOKING YOUR DINNER Things cooking in the oven are almost done when you can smell them in the living room. *Gordon Hard, assistant editor, Consumer Reports*

735. ORGANIZING YOUR GOALS Write down your goals, then see what's happening to them after six months. Throw out the ones you don't care about anymore. Any of the remaining goals that you haven't worked on in six months are not really goals — either you're fooling yourself or you've inherited some "shoulds" that you don't believe in. *Andrea Frankel, computer scientist, engineer, and holistic health practitioner, San Diego, California*

736. CHOOSING A TENNIS OPPONENT Never agree to play tennis for money against a gray-haired player. *Tom Robinson, computer programmer, Berkeley, California*

737. LOOKING AT HOUSES In house building, the lighter the framing, the more recent the construction. *Greg Koos, McLean County Historical Society, Bloomington, Illinois*

738. SQUEEZING GRAPES One ton of grapes makes 120 gallons of wine. *Peter Reimuller, Point Arena, California*

739. WEARING JEWELRY AND MAKE-UP Teenage girls should lay out the jewelry they want to wear, then put away one third of the items. For make-up, they should lay out everything they'd like to use, then put away all but two items. *Tim Hoff, twentieth-century bureaucrat, APO New York*

740. HITCHHIKING WITH BOOKS Each textbook you carry while hitchhiking reduces your wait by five minutes.
Tim Hoff, twentieth-century bureaucrat, APO New York

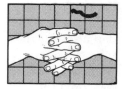

741. ALEX'S RULES OF PORTRAITURE Your portraits won't look so gimpy if you check to be sure the eyes are on a line halfway between the top of the head and the chin; the inside corners of the eyes are one eye-width apart; the nose is almost halfway between the eyes and chin; the nose is as wide as the distance between the eyes; the corners of the mouth fall directly below the pupils of the eyes; the tops of the ears are on eye level; and the bottoms of the ears come between the bottom of the nose and the mouth. *Alex Stewart, Atlanta, Georgia*

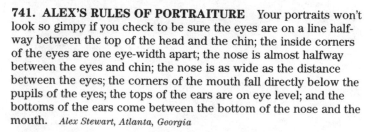

742. TACKLING A PROJECT Bite off more than you can chew. Your mouth is bigger than you think.
Wm. Jeff Lindsay, bicycle designer and builder, Mountain Goat Cycles, Chico, California

743. HOSTING A RADIO TALK SHOW During a radio talk show, at least 1 percent of the callers will phone in with nothing more to say than how hard it is to call the show.
Rob Kersting, WVLK radio, Lexington, Kentucky

744. BAKING BREAD You can safely add two cups of anything to the standard two-loaf bread recipe if you substitute a cup of gluten flour for a cup of all-purpose flour and your dough is well risen before the addition.
Andrea Frankel, computer scientist, engineer, and holistic health practitioner, San Diego, California

745. USING A POOL No more than 10 percent of the people in an apartment complex will try to use the pool at the same time, and about 80 percent will never use it.
Vince Mooney, real estate broker, Tulsa, Oklahoma

746. WRITING A BLURB It takes four times as long to write an effective book jacket blurb that is five words long as it does to write one that is thirty words long. But the shorter copy is seven times better. *Walter Pitkin, literary agent, Weston, Connecticut*

747. TAKING A SHOWER A ten-minute shower is worth an hour and a half of sleep.
Laurie Baldwin, student, Oregon State University

748. MOVING A TREE A truck-mounted tree spade should cut a root ball ten times the diameter of the tree trunk. A tree with a five-inch trunk, for example, should have a root ball fifty inches in diameter. *Dr. George E. Fitzpatrick, Fort Lauderdale, Florida*

You have ninety days to make and ship a novelty item and ninety days to sell it out. After that, inventory costs swallow up the profits.

Ellis E. Conklin, UPI feature writer, quoting Fred Reinstein, fad merchant

749. ADDING AN ECHO   When adding echo to a vocal track, add half again as much as you think you should.
Dick Brenton, record producer

750. PICKING STEEL CABLE   The safe working load of steel cable, in tons, is the diameter in inches squared multiplied by eight. For example, for one-half-inch cable, $\frac{1}{2} \times \frac{1}{2} \times 8 = 2$ tons.
Paul Carter, stagehand, New York City

751. THE STUDENT IS READY RULE   When you're ready to do something about a problem, almost anything can help. When you're not ready, no amount of workshops, counseling, or programs will effect a lasting change. The rule is: When the student is ready, the teacher appears.
Andrea Frankel, computer scientist, engineer, and holistic health practitioner, San Diego, California

752. APPRAISING A RENTAL PROPERTY   The market value of a rental property is six times the gross rent.
Larry Beck, joiner, Lansing, New York

753. DESIGNING A STAGE SET   Check your design for a stage set by squinting your eyes. If any prop or color pops out, tone it down.   *Dean Sheridan, Downey, California*

754. LEARNING MANNERS   You learn half your manners from those who have good manners and half from those who have no manners.   *Fr. Emmet C. Smith, Largo, Florida*

755. EXERCISING IN THE HEAT When exercising in the heat, drop your performance expectations by about 2 percent for every 10° above 55° F. The same 2 percent adjustment works for every thousand feet above altitudes of five thousand feet.
Ned Frederick, writer, Exeter, New Hampshire

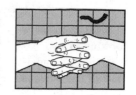

756. ADJUSTING TO HEAT AND ALTITUDE It takes one week to get used to exercising in the heat, but about three weeks to adjust to changes in altitude.
Ned Frederick, writer, Exeter, New Hampshire

757. WATCHING THE WIND AND TIDE On the seashore, the wind rises when the tide changes.
David Lyon, writer and advertising authority, Westport, Connecticut

758. THE RAIN OR SNOW RULE If it is snowing, and tree trunks appear to darken in midday, the snow will change to rain. *Walter Pitkin, literary agent, Weston, Connecticut*

759. THE SECOND RAIN OR SNOW RULE If snow or rain is likely and the air appears gray, it will snow. If it has a bluish haze, expect rain. *Walter Pitkin, literary agent, Weston, Connecticut*

760. PICKING A PROGRAMMER Never hire a computer programmer who knows only one programming language.
Andrea Frankel, computer scientist, engineer, and holistic health practitioner, San Diego, California

761. CHECKING A BLADE Sharp saws and chain saws produce large chips when they cut wood; fine dust means a dull blade. *Pierce Butler, Natchez, Mississippi*

762. FOLLOWING THE SUN AND THE MOON For a given latitude, the path of the full moon across the sky at the summer solstice is approximately the same as the path of the sun at the winter solstice, and vice versa. *Pierce Butler, Natchez, Mississippi*

763. THE DIFFERENCE BETWEEN MEN AND WOMEN
Turn your head to one side and hold the opposite arm out straight in the other direction. The distance from a woman's nose to the tip of her fingertips will be nearly one yard; for a man it will be about a meter. *Isabel T. Coburn, authority at large, Pemaquid Beach, Maine*

764. GETTING THINGS DONE Make a new "to do" list every day from your larger list of projects, goals, and things to do. If an item gets transferred from one daily list to the next for ten days, drop it. There's a reason you're avoiding the item, and your time would be better spent reassessing your motives.
Andrea Frankel, computer scientist, engineer, and holistic health practitioner, San Diego, California

JON REIS

765. CHANGING YOUR ANSWERS The closer you are to running out of time, the less you should mess with your essay answers. When you change a sentence on an essay test, other sentences need to be changed as well.
Dean Sheridan, Downey, California

766. BREAKING BOLTS AND STUDS If a bolt breaks while you are screwing it in, you will be able to remove the broken piece, but if it breaks while you are unscrewing it, forget trying to remove the broken piece. Drill it out and retap the threads.
Chris Packard, The Packard Company, Newton Centre, Massachusetts

767. RENTING A VIDEOTAPE Never rent a videotape from a store to which it will be inconvenient to return it.
Chris Packard, The Packard Company, Newton Centre, Massachusetts

768. PAINTING YOUR COOP If you paint the inside of your chicken coop orange, your chickens will lay more eggs.
Diana Souza, illustrator, Ithaca, New York

769. CLEANING A BATHROOM No matter how fast you think you can do it, it takes one hour to thoroughly clean a bathroom. *John Towle, Salinas, California*

770. ATTRACTING JUNK MAIL For every magazine or newspaper you subscribe to, you will receive at least five pieces of junk mail per month. *John Towle, Salinas, California*

771. REBUILDING YOUR FAUCETS When you first think about how hard it is to turn a faucet, it's time to rebuild it.
Mitch Doll, builder, Brooktondale, New York

772. PLANTING CORN IN BERKS COUNTY, PA. To avoid frost damage, plant your corn when the maple leaves are the size of mouse ears. *Sigmund Sameth, Irvington, New Jersey*

773. FOLLOWING A DEER If deer droppings are black, moist, and glossy, the deer left them within fifteen or twenty minutes and is in the immediate vicinity. If the droppings are no longer glossy, they have been on the ground for an hour or more and the deer is probably bedded down on a southern slope. Deer droppings that are gray were left the day before.
Sigmund Sameth, Irvington, New Jersey

774. CHECKING THE WIND FROM THE AIR If you're in an airplane and you can't find any waving flags or smoke plumes to indicate the wind direction on the ground, check the way the cows are facing. Cows prefer to face away from the wind when they're grazing and when they're lying on the ground chewing their cuds. *Sigmund Sameth, Irvington, New Jersey*

775. THE 80/20/30 RULE If you get rid of the 20 percent of your customers who cause 80 percent of your headaches, your profits will increase by 30 percent. *Alex Stewart, Atlanta, Georgia*

776. DRIVING IN THE MOUNTAINS When driving in the mountains, brake before you reach a curve, then accelerate as you drive into the curve. You should always be able to stop in the distance you can see. *Alex Stewart, Atlanta, Georgia*

777. LOUISE'S RULE OF CHRISTMAS A white Christmas means a black cemetery. *Louise Pearson, Burlington, Iowa*

778. TESTING FOR EDIBILITY If you are foraging for food but are not sure about the edibility of a plant, take a small amount in your mouth, chew it, and hold it there without swallowing for five minutes. If you feel no ill effects — such as stinging, burning, or numbness — swallow it and then wait for eight hours. If by that time you have not experienced any cramps, pain, numbing, vomiting, or diarrhea, eat another handful of the plant and wait another eight hours. If there is still no problem, consider the plant safe to eat.
Michael Rozek, reporting on the Air Force Survival School in <u>National Wildlife</u>

779. TESTING YOUR SCRIMSHAW Test your scrimshaw by touching the surface of the tooth with a red-hot needle. If it smokes, it's plastic. If it doesn't smoke, make sure the tooth is hollow from the base to the tip; fake scrimshaw is hollow only partway up. *Susan J. Macovsky, writer,* <u>Money</u>

> No matter how fast you think you can do it, it takes one hour to thoroughly clean a bathroom.
>
> *John Towle, Salinas, California*

780. WATCHING A YACHT RACE Body english reveals a lot about a yacht racing tactician. When you see a tactician with his hands in his pockets, he's relaxed and comfortable with the way the race is going. When you see him with his hands folded across his chest, he's a little bit concerned. When his hands are on his hips, he's getting worried.

Gary Jobsen, yacht racing tactician and twelve meter specialist, on ESPN's America's Cup coverage

781. THE DUTCH RULE FOR RAIN If the birds are out in the rain, the rain will continue for the rest of the day.

Dirck Z. Meengs, management consultant, Canoga Park, California

782. ADDRESSING SOMEONE'S PERSONAL SPACE If the person you're talking to keeps moving closer, making you feel crowded, assume that he needs a smaller personal space than you, and hold your ground. Then if he stops moving in on you, you've made the right decision, and things will go better, provided you can master your own feeling of being hemmed in. Conversely, if the person you're talking to keeps backing up, assume that he needs a bigger personal space than you, and stop trying to get closer.   *Suzette Haden Elgin, author of The Gentle Art of Verbal Self-Defense*

783. RAISING SWINE It takes the profit from four pigs to pay the cost of keeping a sow. The fifth pig is the first one that makes you money.   *Julius E. Nordby, author of Swine*

784. DEFINING INSIDER TRADING If an investor even suspects that a stock tip is based on insider information and that the stock price would be affected if the public knew about it, it probably is illegal for him to trade in the stock.
Gary Lynch, director of enforcement, Securities and Exchange Commission, in the New York Times

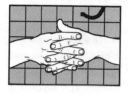

785. BUYING A FUR Buy the best fur in a breed that you can afford. If your limit is $3,000, consider a fine beaver instead of a so-so mink. *Eloise Salholz, Savvy*

786. CORRELATING BRAIN DAMAGE TO IQ Among brain-damaged children who were five years old or older when their brain damage occurred, each 1 percent of brain tissue destroyed means a four-point drop in IQ. *Laurence Miller, Psychology Today*

787. POURING A SLAB Control joints in a concrete slab should be cut to a depth of one fourth of the slab's thickness.
William C. Panarese, manager, Building Technology Department, Portland Cement Association, in Popular Science

788. WATCHING CANADA GEESE The farther north you go, the smaller the geese; the farther west, the darker the color.
Mary Ellen Parker, teacher, Cincinnati, Ohio

789. FIGHTING GUERRILLA SOLDIERS To fight a guerrilla army, a national army needs ten soldiers for every one guerrilla.
Dr. Constantine Menges, special assistant to the President for national security affairs, on National Public Radio

790. SUING FOR MEDICAL EXPENSES Three times the medical expenses is a reasonable amount to sue for in a court of law. *Judge Wapner, TV judge, "People's Court"*

791. WATCHING THE WEATHER When rain or snow starts light and slow, it will last a long time; when it starts quick and is heavy, it won't last long.
Robert Hastings, master chief petty officer, U.S. Coast Guard

792. COUNTING ROACHES Set a roach trap and check it after twenty-four hours. For every roach you've caught in your trap, you've got eight hundred more in your kitchen. If you find more than one or two in your trap, you have a serious roach problem.
Richard S. Patterson, entomologist, in The Washington Post Weekly

793. LOOKING AT FROZEN FOOD On a package of frozen food, if it takes longer to read the ingredients than to cook it in a microwave, choose another product.
Susanna Levin, assistant editor, New Age Journal

To determine where the sidewalks for a new building on campus should be, construct the building without sidewalks and wait for one year. Then put the sidewalks on the paths the students have made.

Larry Morgan and Fred Fry, Kansas City, Missouri

794. COMPARING THE PRICE OF GOLD TO OIL Under ideal conditions, the price of an ounce of gold should equal the price of thirteen barrels of oil. *Anonymous expert*

795. BALANCING WEIGHT AGAINST SALARY Fat corporate executives earn less money. Each pound you are overweight costs you about $1,000 a year in salary.
Dr. Albert Stunkard, psychiatrist and obesity expert, quoted in the Syracuse Post-Standard

796. MAKING A SPECULATIVE INVESTMENT Speculative investments, such as silver, should never exceed 10 percent of your investment portfolio. *Merrie Spaeth, USA Weekend*

797. LOSING BEACHES Along the East Coast of the United States, a one-foot rise in sea level moves beach erosion one hundred feet inland.
Dr. Stephen P. Leatherman, associate professor of geomorphology, University of Maryland, in the New York Times

798. MASSAGING AN INJURED AREA Don't heat or massage an injury if, when you hold your hand one-half inch from the skin, you can feel more heat in the injured area than in the surrounding area.
Andrea Frankel, computer scientist, engineer, and holistic health practitioner, San Diego, California

799. SIZING-UP THE REAL ESTATE MARKET To size-up an area's real estate market, compare the difference between the original asking price and the final selling price on recent home sales. A difference of 1 to 4 percent means it's a seller's market. A difference greater than 5 percent means it's a buyer's market.
Susan Bondy, financial columnist, News America Syndicate

800. SAVING MONEY You should budget your money so that you can put 10 to 15 percent of your earnings into savings.
Merrie Spaeth, USA Weekend

801. WATERING THE GRASS It's time to water your lawn when the grass has a purplish cast and when footprints remain after walking across the lawn, a sign of wilting.
Norman W. Hummel, Jr., assistant professor, New York State College of Agriculture and Life Sciences at Cornell University, in the Ithaca Journal

802. SIZING-UP A SCHOOL PROGRAM The more trivial a school program, the more pretentious the jargon used to justify it.
Emery Nemethy, Catawissa, Pennsylvania

803. TALKING TO BABIES Too much talking can overstimulate your baby, while too little can leave your child quiet and unresponsive. The optimum amount of time for baby talk is 25 to 30 percent of the time your infant is alert and responsive. If your baby is alert for half an hour, limit talk to seven to ten minutes.
Marilyn Elias, quoting UCLA child psychologist Kiki V. Roe, in American Health

804. PLANNING A PARKING LOT If you are designing a parking lot, plan on three hundred square feet per vehicle.
Dirck Z. Meengs, management consultant, Canoga Park, California

805. DETERMINING THE AGE OF A SPRUCE TREE You can determine the approximate age of a spruce tree by counting the layers of limbs on its trunk. A tree that has ten layers of limbs is roughly ten years old.
Thomas O. Marsh, writer and amateur naturalist, Fairfield, Ohio

806. SYNDICATING A TV SERIES A television series needs to have been produced for three years, or have eighty episodes, before it is an attractive candidate for daily syndication.
John Efroymson and Malinda Runyan, media analysts, Arlington, Virginia

807. FEEDING KIDS Children don't need huge servings of food. Start with one tablespoon of each item per year of age.
Gayle Peterson, mother, Columbus, Ohio

808. ESTIMATING THE CALORIE CONTENT OF FOODS Solid foods high in carbohydrates and protein contain about one hundred calories per ounce. Fatty foods contain about two hundred calories per ounce.
Ned Frederick, writer, Exeter, New Hampshire

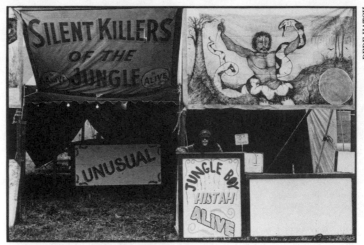

DEDE HATCH

809. KEEPING YOUR CUSTOMERS #1   For every complaint
a company receives, there are twenty-six other customers with
problems, and six are serious.
Technical Assistant Research Programs, in Microservice Management

810. KEEPING YOUR CUSTOMERS #2   Complainers are
more likely than dissatisfied noncomplainers to do business again
with the company that upset them, even if the problem is not sat-
isfactorily resolved.
Technical Assistance Research Programs, in Microservice Management

811. KEEPING YOUR CUSTOMERS #3   Between 54 and 70
percent of customers who complain to a company will do business with the company again if their complaint was resolved. That
figure increases to 95 percent if the customer feels the complaint
was resolved quickly.
Technical Assistance Research Programs, in Microservice Management

812. CHOOSING FABRIC FOR CLOTHING   Texture and
sheen look bigger; smooth and dull look smaller. This is why most
of us should never appear in public in tight pink satin jeans.
Donna Salyers, Cincinnati Enquirer

813. WATCHING YOUR HEART RATE   Your maximum safe
heart rate is equal to 220 minus your age. For example, a forty-
year-old would have a maximum heart rate of $220 - 40 = 180$
beats per minute. Your target heart rate for aerobic exercise is
equal to 160 minus your age. That's the number of beats per minute you need to maintain or exceed during aerobic workouts.
Ned Frederick, writer, Exeter, New Hampshire

814. INCREASING YOUR AEROBIC FITNESS To increase your aerobic fitness, get your heart rate above your target rate for at least ninety minutes a week.
Ned Frederick, writer, Exeter, New Hampshire

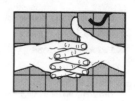

815. REFINANCING A HOME Homeowners should think about refinancing their homes if market rates drop two or three percentage points below their mortgage rate.
David Lane, Lincoln, Nebraska

816. REFINANCING YOUR HOME It makes sense to refinance a home mortgage if the money you save with the lower interest rate pays for the cost of refinancing within three years.
John T. Reed's Real Estate Investor's Monthly

817. LISTENING TO BIRDS When birds — especially bluejays — seem to chatter more than usual, expect a storm within twenty-four hours. *Virginia Williams, Burlington, Iowa*

818. SIZING-UP A PATIENT If a patient is proud of claiming that no physician has been able to diagnose what is wrong with him, don't plan on being the first doctor to break his record.
Gerry M. Flick, M.D., ship's surgeon, S.S. Constitution

819. CATCHING SHOPLIFTERS Shoplifters are most active on Fridays and Sundays between three P.M. and six P.M.
Roger Griffin, retail security agency official, Van Nuys, California, in Parade

820. STORING IMPORTANT DOCUMENTS Every ten degrees you lower the temperature of stored documents will double their life. *Jan Rich, journalist, Austin, Texas*

821. CHECKING YOUR WATER FOR HARDNESS You can tell if your water is hard or soft by looking at your ice cubes. Hard-water cubes have a white spot in the center where minerals congregate; soft-water cubes are uniformly cloudy.
Lou J. Smith, executive director, Canadian Water Quality Association, in the Houston Chronicle

822. ESTIMATING A CONSTRUCTION JOB If a construction estimator wins a bid and it is within 10 percent of the next lowest bid, it means he probably will make money on the job and he didn't underestimate the costs.
Harvey Mitchell, construction estimator, Beaumont, Texas

823. THE STAR RULE Stars twinkle, planets don't.
Scott Parker, Beaumont, Texas

824. OVEREATING The first time it occurs to you that you have eaten enough, you have.
Andrea Frankel, computer scientist, engineer, and holistic health practitioner, San Diego, California

825. SPOTTING A DRUNK   If someone wipes his mouth right after taking a drink, he has probably been overindulging.
Scott Parker, Beaumont, Texas

826. SPEAKING FRENCH IN ENGLISH   One in twenty words and phrases spoken in everyday French is actually English.   *"The Story of English" on PBS, hosted by Robert MacNeil*

827. ADJUSTING THE SIGHTS ON A RIFLE   If your rifle has more zip than a .30-30 and you sight it to hit a couple of inches above the point of aim at one hundred yards, it will put most bullets close to the bull's-eye at two hundred yards.
Shannon Tompkins, columnist, Beaumont (Texas) Enterprise

828. UPDATING CORPORATE COMPUTERS   In most large organizations, the computers are ten years out of date and the programs for those computers are twenty years out of date. Attempts by these organizations to "modernize" only succeed in maintaining this lag — by the time an organization has decided to install a state of the art system, it is no longer state of the art, and it will often be shackled to the older equipment. Recognition of this fact accounts for much of the success of IBM.
Phil A. Schrodt, associate professor, Northwestern University

829. TALKING ABOUT YOUR CHILD   A child will become as you describe him to others.   *Attributed to Danny Kaye*

830. STOCKING AN ICE CREAM TRUCK The most successful ice cream trucks are the ones that stock items in a wide range of prices, from one penny up, because children do not like to get change back. *Ellen Klaver, musician, Boulder, Colorado*

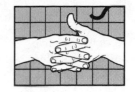

831. TESTING BREAD DOUGH To test your bread dough, poke two holes in it as deep as the first joint of your thumb. If the holes are still there after thirty seconds, it has risen enough.
Andrea Frankel, computer scientist, engineer, and holistic health practitioner, San Diego, California

832. WATCHING HORSES LOOK You can get an idea of what horses are looking at by watching the position of their heads. Horses lower their heads to see objects in the distance. They raise their heads to see objects up close.
George Huebner, Houston Chronicle

833. SHINING UP YOUR HORSE A horse with a dull coat needs more corn in its diet. *George Huebner, Houston Chronicle*

834. PAYING FOR HORSES The average cost to maintain a horse is $1,000 a year on pasture and almost $4,000 at a stable.
George Huebner, Houston Chronicle

835. INKING A RUBBER STAMP The finer the detail on a rubber stamp, the less ink it takes and the easier it is to get a good impression.
Alan T. Whittemore, YMCA director, South Deerfield, Massachusetts

836. CHOOSING A MATTRESS The amount you move during sleep is directly proportional to the hardness of your mattress. Generally, then, the greater the back problem, the harder your mattress should be. The unforgiving surface forces you to move often, and your muscles won't become stiff from lack of movement. *Alan T. Whittemore, YMCA director, South Deerfield, Massachusetts*

837. LISTENING TO YOUR ENGINE KNOCK If your engine knocks during acceleration, it's probably the connecting rod. If the engine knocks during deceleration, it's probably the piston wrist pin. If you have piston slap (too much room between the piston and the cylinder wall), the knock will be loudest when the engine is cold and idling. *Ray Hill, car care columnist*

838. FEEDING COCKROACHES Twelve cockroaches can live on the glue of a postage stamp for a week.
Austin Friedman, entomologist

839. IDENTIFYING GEESE If geese are flying in a close V formation, they are almost certainly Canada geese. If they form a looser V, rippling and waving, or if they are in a long line like one leg of a V, they are more likely the less common snow geese.
Hal Borland's Book of Days

JON CRISPIN

840. LEANING A LADDER When you use an extension ladder, you should put the bottom of the ladder one foot away from the wall for every four feet of vertical height.
Scott M. Kruse, biogeographer, Fresno, California

841. DONATING SPACE FOR ANNOUNCEMENTS People looking for free newspaper space for announcements typically want them to run more than once. Follow the old newspaper rule: One announcement is news, two announcements is advertising.
Ben Hansen, editor, Beaumont (Texas) Enterprise

842. DODGING DRUNK DRIVERS On Friday and Saturday nights, one in ten cars coming toward you has a drunk driver behind the wheel. *Scott Parker, Beaumont, Texas, quoting Parade*

843. LOSING WEIGHT #1 You lose a pound of fat for every 3,500 calories you burn or don't eat.
Ned Frederick, writer, Exeter, New Hampshire

844. LOSING WEIGHT #2 Don't try to lose more than two pounds per week. More than that is too much too soon.
Ned Frederick, writer, Exeter, New Hampshire

845. LOSING WEIGHT WHILE GAINING AGE You should lose one pound of body weight every three years after age thirty to offset the increase in body fat that accompanies aging.
Ned Frederick, writer, Exeter, New Hampshire

846. USING A COMPOSTING OUTHOUSE   When using a fifty-five-gallon drum as a receptacle in a composting outhouse, where you add a good scoop of hay or wood shavings after each use, six people will fill one drum in about six weeks.
Pierce Butler, Natchez, Mississippi

847. BOOK PUBLISHING   If you ask a publisher if a new book is selling well, and she replies, "It's too soon to tell" — it isn't — and it isn't.   *Walter Pitkin, literary agent, Weston, Connecticut*

848. THE EFFECT OF WATER ON TEMPERATURE   During the summer, as you move inland from a large body of water, the temperature will increase 1° F per mile for the first ten miles. During the winter, the temperature will decrease accordingly.
Dirck Z. Meengs, management consultant, Canoga Park, California

849. BUYING A USED BOOK   If a used book store has more than one copy of a book written before 1975, it will be worth your while to check each one. The cover prices will probably differ.
Bruce Reznick, associate professor of mathematics, Urbana, Illinois

850. RETAIL MARKETING   You should figure it will take three months for an effective retail marketing campaign to take hold.   *Scott Parker, Beaumont, Texas*

851. THE BANKING RULE OF 3/3/3   Pay 3 percent for your money. Charge 3 percent more than that for loans. Get out on the golf course by 3 P.M.   *Scott Parker, Beaumont, Texas*

852. TALKING WITH HEADPHONES ON   When speaking while wearing headphones, don't try to hear your own voice; try to feel a familiar level of vibration in your throat.
Tom Robinson, computer programmer, Berkeley, California

853. UPSTAGING SOMEONE   The more another performer is upstaging you, the fewer moves you should make. The audience is more fascinated with the leaning palm tree than with the hurricane.   *Dean Sheridan, Downey, California*

854. RAISING YOUR HAND   When a teacher needs someone to volunteer an answer, raise your hand at the same time as the class genius. If you time it right, neither of you will be picked.
Dean Sheridan, Downey, California

855. DIGGING A GRAVE   The standard size of a human grave is 7'8" long by 3'2" wide by 6' deep, unless there is to be more than one person buried in it. Then add 2 feet of depth for each body.   *Rev. Halsey DeW. Howe, Saint Mark's Church, Springfield, Vermont*

For every magazine or newspaper you subscribe to, you will receive at least five pieces of junk mail per month.

John Towle, Salinas, California

856. IMPORTING PARROTS   Only one in fifty parrots taken from the wild survives to live in a private home.
Scott Parker, Beaumont, Texas

857. THE RULE OF FLIGHT   Two out of three living critters can fly.   *L. M. Boyd, San Francisco Chronicle*

858. J. MAC McCLELLAN'S WINTER FLYING RULE   If it is daylight, and the weather along your route is at least a one-thousand-foot ceiling and three miles visibility, and you find icing so heavy that your airplane cannot continue to fly, you probably can crash-land the airplane under control and survive. If the clouds are lower, the visibility less, or if it is after dark, you simply shouldn't take off into likely icing conditions without de-icing equipment on your plane.   *J. Mac McClellan, senior editor, Flying*

859. TAKING OFF IN A PLANE   A good minimum runway length for a light airplane is double the manufacturer's recommended distance needed to climb to fifty feet.
J. Mac McClellan, senior editor, Flying

860. CHOOSING A GAMBLING PARTNER   You will almost always gamble better if you gamble alone.
Marvin Karlins, Ph.D., gambling authority and author of Psyching-Out Vegas

861. KNOWING WHEN TO QUIT GAMBLING End any gambling session after winning half your session's stake. If you start a session with $2,000, quit when you reach $3,000. You can ride out a hot streak, but as soon as you lose one bet, it's time to quit, convert your profits to traveler's checks, and mail them home.
Marvin Karlins, Ph.D., gambling authority and author of Psyching-Out Vegas

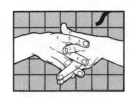

862. BRUSHING YOUR TEETH Get a new toothbrush as soon as your old one gets frayed. If you're not going through four toothbrushes a year, you're not brushing your teeth enough.
Gerald Gutlipp, mathematician, Chicago, Illinois

863. BUILDING GIANT RETAIL STORES Huge food stores are increasing in number, but per-store sales have been declining since 1983. That's because people are getting fed up with the time it takes to shop in warehouse-size stores. Typically, these stores have 100,000 square feet of food and merchandise but customers start reaching the limits of their patience and endurance at about 60,000 to 65,000 square feet of store.
Willard Bishop, economist, in Marketing News

864. CARING FOR A SICK CHILD If your child is four months old or younger and is running a rectal temperature greater than 100° F, get medical help.
Scott M. Kruse, biogeographer, and Martha Betcher, medical technologist, Fresno, California

865. MAINTAINING YOUR WEIGHT To calculate the calories you need daily to maintain your weight, multiply your weight by ten. *Dr. Robin Kanarek, in Tufts University Diet and Nutrition Letter*

866. STICKING WITH A FITNESS PROGRAM If you can follow a fitness program for twenty-one consecutive days, you can follow it for life. *Kenneth Blanchard, author, quoted in Boardroom Reports*

867. CHOOSING A PUPPY If a dog tolerates gentle handling between its toes, it probably is suited for children.
The Pets Are Wonderful Council

868. BUYING AND SELLING STOCK You're trading too much if you turn over an average of more than one third of your portfolio each year. *Gerald W. Perritt, editor, Investment Horizons*

869. UNDERSTANDING FRENCH PHILOSOPHY To understand modern French philosophy, simply assume that everything intangible is real, while everything material is unreal. Thus, disappointment is real, but your Citroën is not.
Gordon Hard, assistant editor, Consumer Reports

When trying on glasses, put them on and look at your feet. If they start to slip off your face, they are too loose.

Paul Lampe, writer and poet, St. Louis, Missouri

870. GETTING SOMETHING FIXED Items that originally cost less than $50 are rarely worth repairing. It's usually cheaper to buy a new one. *Glamour, quoted in Bottom Line/Personal*

871. ASSEMBLING NEW THINGS The fact that the label on a box claims that what's inside can be assembled without tools has no bearing on whether you'll need them or not.
Mark McMullen, accountant, Alexandria, Virginia

872. TAKING A LOSS When you've lost 10 percent on an investment, take your losses and get out.
Paul Lisseck, flower photographer, Ithaca, New York

873. MAKING A PORT OF CALL Count on spending $40 to $50 each day you are in a port, to cover tips, drinks, tours, and taxi fares. Shopping is extra.
Travel Smart, Communications House, Inc., Dobbs Ferry, New York

874. RAISING YOUR SALARY When negotiating your salary with a recruiter, make your opening figure at least 30 percent higher than your present pay package (including bonuses, perks, and your next raise). If the new job will involve moving to a larger city or to the Northeast or West Coast, add another 10 percent.
Charles Fleming, author of Executive Pursuit

875. RENTING APARTMENTS Unless you get a name and phone number, half the people who make appointments to see rental property won't show up.
Vince Mooney, real estate broker, Tulsa, Oklahoma

876. THINKING ABOUT CALIFORNIA The more someone dislikes Californians, the more likely he or she is from an eastern state. The more extreme the dislike, the more likely he or she is from Ohio.
Edward J. Garrison, nursing home administrator, Watsonville, California

877. PRODUCING A VIDEOTAPE Figure on spending about $1,000 for every minute of finished high-quality videotape.
Garth V. Gentilin, video expert, New York City

878. PERFORMING BLUEGRASS In bluegrass music, the most tasteless licks, especially on the banjo, get the best response. *Ellen Klaver, musician, Boulder, Colorado*

879. RECRUITING AT COLLEGES Company recruiters should aim to hire at least one student for every school they visit. Not hiring anyone virtually guarantees a thinner response at the school the following year.
William J. McBurney, Jr., management consultant, New York City

880. USING ENERGY IN BUILDINGS Most buildings waste 40 percent of their energy. For example, you never use 30 percent of the hot water you pay for; chalk it up to heat loss in the tank and plumbing. *Mary Welch, Orange Park, Florida*

881. SIZING-UP A CALCULUS TEXT The longer a calculus textbook, the less it covers.
Bruce Reznick, associate professor of mathematics, Urbana, Illinois

882. MANAGING YOUR PERSONAL DEBT Your monthly mortgage payments (principal, interest, taxes, and insurance) should not exceed 28 percent of your gross monthly salary. The payments for your mortgage and consumer loans combined should not exceed 35 percent of your gross salary.
Jane Bryant Quinn in Woman's Day, cited in Bottom Line/Personal

883. WORKING WITH SCIENCE PROFESSORS Science professors are notorious misspellers. Correct them whenever your grade point average is low. *Dean Sheridan, Downey, California*

884. BETTING ON A BASEBALL GAME Bet on any pitcher who starts on his birthday. Bet on any starter who is pitching on the road but happens to be in his home town.
George Ignatin, professor of economics, University of Alabama at Birmingham

885. BANKING ADVICE FOR SMALL BUSINESSES Consider a new bank if the one you now use changes your loan officer and the new officer doesn't visit you within thirty days. You should also consider a switch if the bank changes your loan officer twice in one year. *Robert Kahn, editor, Retailing Today*

JON CRISPIN

886. CHECKING YOUR EXHAUST   Blue smoke from your exhaust may mean your car needs a complete engine overhaul. Black smoke usually means a maladjusted carburetor. Ignore white smoke if the engine is cold, but if it keeps up after the engine has warmed, you may have a leaking head gasket.
Reader's Digest, reported in Bottom Line/Personal

887. HUGGING SOMEONE Four hugs a day is the minimum needed to meet a person's "skin hunger."
Greg Risberg, clinical social worker, Northwestern University Medical School

888. STRUGGLING WITH ALGEBRA Repeating Algebra 1 rarely raises the grade by more than one letter — for example, from C to B, or D to C. *R. C. Woods, teacher, Miranda, California*

889. HAVING AN ADVENTURE Adventure is not fun while it's happening. *Peter Reimuller, Point Arena, California*

890. DRINKING WINE Wine before a meal increases hunger. Wine during a meal quells the appetite. Wine at the end of a meal can drown the desire for dessert.
Maria Simonson, Ph.D., Sc.D., Johns Hopkins Medical Institutions, Good Samaritan Hospital

891. ESTIMATING YOUR BLOOD VOLUME You can estimate the volume of blood in your body if you know your weight. Your weight in kilograms multiplied by .08 equals your blood volume in liters. *Ned Frederick, writer, Exeter, New Hampshire*

892. FITTING A SHOE You should have a thumb's width of space between the longest toe and the tip of your shoe.
Charles J. Gudas, D.P.M., professor of clinical surgery, University of Chicago Medical Center

893. DEALING WITH FRIGHTENED DOGS A stray dog who is afraid of people will trust the owners of the dogs it plays with.
Andrea Frankel, computer scientist, engineer, and holistic health practitioner, San Diego, California

894. USING A SAUNA Bathing in a sauna for only fifteen minutes uses up as many calories as a mile or two of jogging.
Bottom Line/Personal

895. PLANTING CONIFER SEEDLINGS Two people equipped with mattocks or dibble bars can plant eight hundred to one thousand conifer seedlings in a day, if no beer is served before noon. *Joe Schwartz, editor, Danby, New York*

896. ENJOYING YOUR VACATION You will have more fun on your vacation if you maintain a mental age of eighteen or less. Act just old enough to make your travel connections and stay out of trouble. *Joe Schwartz, editor, Danby, New York*

897. DEVELOPING REAL ESTATE Barring geographic barriers, cities will grow, and grow affluent, toward the northwest.
Michael Ridley, real estate developer, El Paso, Texas, quoted by Alan Weisman in La Frontera

New motorcyclists get cocky and reckless when they've put three thousand miles, or the equivalent of one trip across the United States, on their bikes.

"Wolfman," Hell's Angel, Natchez, Mississippi

DEDE HATCH

898. MARRYING A DOCTOR   If a doctor sets up practice in a town with one-fifth or less the population of the town his or her spouse was raised in, they will divorce or move to a larger town within five years.   *Gerry M. Flick, M.D., ship's surgeon, S.S. Constitution*

899. TALKING TO CAB DRIVERS   If a taxi driver talks a lot, let him. If he doesn't talk, don't ask him to. And if he laughs all the time, never ask him why.
Mark McMullen, accountant, Alexandria, Virginia

900. GLAZING A BUTCHER SHOP   If you have a butcher shop with raw meat on display, the greener the glass in the window, the more the flies will stay away. Unfortunately, it has the same effect on customers.   *Diana Souza, illustrator, Ithaca, New York*

901. SELLING CONSTRUCTION EQUIPMENT   Construction equipment dealers make 75 percent of their profits repairing and servicing equipment already in the field.
Scott Parker, Beaumont, Texas

902. WATCHING A BUSINESS START   If a recently opened store spreads its inventory thin by devoting a large amount of shelf space to each product, the owner is showing a healthy caution by not investing heavily before he has developed a clientele and a knowledge of his customers.
Walter Pitkin, literary agent, Weston, Connecticut

903. WATCHING A BUSINESS STOP   If an older store begins to spread its stock thin, and especially if it seems to feature old inventory, it is in serious distress and is likely to fail.
Walter Pitkin, literary agent, Weston, Connecticut

904. FOLLOWING FARMERS   Every six farmers that go broke take a rural business with them.
Cally Arthur, managing editor, Alpine, New York

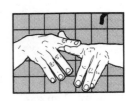

905. WATCHING YOUR WOODSTOVE   When your woodstove is going full bore, you should be able to hold your hand firmly pressed on any nearby combustible surface. If you can't, you need to increase the clearance between the surface and the stove, or install a heat shield.
Peter R. Lammert, Thomaston, Maine, in Blair & Ketchum's Country Journal

906. FINDING TYPOGRAPHICAL ERRORS   Cheap paperback novels average one typographical error for every ten pages.
Joe Applegate, typo hunter, Los Angeles, as reported by Fred T. Shuster, Associated Press

907. DESIGNING A STREET   A city street is most visually appealing if its width is the same as the height of the buildings along it.   *David and Penny Russell, Dilltown, Pennsylvania*

908. SWIMMING FOR EXERCISE   A swimmer needs to exert less energy than a runner to get the same aerobic benefit, because his body is in a horizontal position and his heart pumps more blood per beat than it does when his body is upright. To calculate your ideal heart rate while swimming, subtract your age from 205 and multiply by .70. If your rate is higher than 205 minus your age times .85, you're working harder than you have to.
William McArdle, exercise physiologist, in American Health

909. WRITING A SPORTS BOOK   The sales success of a sports book is inversely proportional to the size of the ball used in the sport.
Frank Deford, senior editor, Sports Illustrated, quoting George Plimpton on "Morning Edition," National Public Radio

910. CHOOSING YOUR GAME   Never make a bet when the house advantage is more than 1.5 percent. In U.S. casinos, this means you can play blackjack, baccarat, and craps, but nothing else.
Marvin Karlins, Ph.D., gambling authority and author of Psyching-Out Vegas

911. SETTING TYPE #1   Avoid setting type in lines of more than sixty-five characters. Longer lines cause the reader to "double," or read the same line twice.   *Peter Smith, Peter Smith Associates*

912. SETTING TYPE #2   Avoid setting type in lines of less than thirty-five characters. Shorter lines cause sentences to be broken and hard to understand.   *Peter Smith, Peter Smith Associates*

The standard size for a human grave is 7'8" long by 3'2" wide by 6' deep, unless there is to be more than one person buried in it. Then add 2 feet of depth for each body.

Rev. Halsey DeW. Howe, Saint Mark's Church, Springfield, Vermont

913. SETTING TYPE #3 Avoid setting type in all capital letters. Capital letters slow reading speed and take 30 percent more space than lowercase letters. *Peter Smith, Peter Smith Associates*

914. INDEXING An average index has three to five entries for each page of text. A light index has one to two entries. A scholarly or technical index has ten entries per page.
Bill Kaupe, consultant, Philadelphia, Pennsylvania

915. FINDING A NUDE BEACH If you face the ocean on a beach where the bathers wear suits, the nude beaches will be to your left more often than to your right.
Gustav Lorentzen, Paradis, Norway

916. STALKING A HOUSEFLY If you're more than three feet away from a housefly, it can't see you.
L. M. Boyd, San Francisco Chronicle

917. MAKING A TELESCOPE For a first-time telescope maker, it is faster to make a four-inch mirror and then a six-inch mirror than it is to make just a six-inch mirror.
Bill McKeeman, Wang Institute, in Communications of the ACM

918. AMASSING A RECORD COLLECTION You will not tire of your record collection if you have two hundred or more albums. *Rusty Cartmill, student newspaper editor, University of Georgia*

919. DEVELOPING GOOD JUDGMENT   Good judgment comes from experience, and experience comes from bad judgment.
Fred Brooks, University of North Carolina, in Communications of the ACM

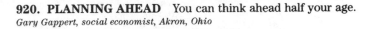

920. PLANNING AHEAD   You can think ahead half your age.
Gary Gappert, social economist, Akron, Ohio

921. SPOTTING AN INSIDE JOB   All large-scale crime is an inside job.   *Slim Pickens, actor, in the film* Rancho Deluxe

922. SPOTTING A MOUSE   If you think you saw a mouse, you did.   *Cheryl Russell, editor in chief,* American Demographics

923. WATCHING HOT DOGS   Throw out hot dogs when the liquid in the package becomes cloudy.
Zak Mettger, writer and vegetarian, Washington, D.C.

924. CHOOSING A POOL CUE   Hold a nickel next to the tip of your pool cue. The tip of the cue is the right shape if its silhouette matches the curve of the nickel's edge.
Michael Rider, art director, Ithaca, New York

925. CHOOSING A PIECE OF MEAT   If there is blood in a package of supermarket meat, the piece is less than fresh.
Brad Edmondson, writer, Ithaca, New York

926. TRAVELING OVERSEAS   Don't travel with anything you can't carry at a dead run for a half mile.
Christopher S. Wren, foreign correspondent, New York Times

927. DRESSING WELL   The fewer the clothes, the more expensive they should look.
Christopher S. Wren, foreign correspondent, New York Times

928. SETTING FENCE POSTS   Extra-large fence posts do not increase the strength of fence corners much, but doubling the depth of a corner post makes it four times stronger.
C. A. Fuller, Sioux Falls, South Dakota

929. SOLVING A JIGSAW PUZZLE   Finding the edge pieces is the first step in assembling a jigsaw puzzle, but finding all of them can be a waste of time. You've spent enough time looking for edge pieces when you've found all four corners.
John Yntema, biologist, Wheeling, West Virginia

930. PROOFREADING   Two rounds of proofreading catch 98 percent of the errors in a book.
Bill Kaupe, consultant, Philadelphia, Pennsylvania

INDEX

This is really two indexes in one. There are specific entries to help you find a particular rule of thumb, and there are general entries (in capital letters) that list large, more whimsical groups of rules that resemble each other for one reason or another. In the mood for some truly awful poetry? Look up RULES THAT RHYME.

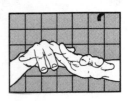

Calories, 493, 494, 567, 660, 808, 843, 865, 894
Camels, 177, 178
Camping, 363
Canned food, 280
Capillary action, 492
Carbohydrates, 808
Carburetion, 98
Carpentry, 463, 502, 515, 653, 659, 673
Casinos, 910
Casseroles, 481, 532
Catalogues, 537
Catering, 388
Cats, 5
Cattle, 664, 665
Cereal, 58
Cesarean sections, 117
Chairs, 621
Champagne, 262, 263, 352, 675
Chandeliers, 101
Charcoal, 14, 156
Charity, 648, 841
Checks, 617
Cheerios, 58
Cheese, 40, 41
Chest pain, 454
Chickadees, 303, 339
Chicken coops, 768
Chickens, 14, 484, 768
Childbirth, 117, 118, 168, 246, 402, 691, 692, 693, 694, 695
Children
  child support, 604
  computers, 612
  discipline, 368
  education, 313, 803, 829
  eyelashes, 150
  health, 57, 483, 786, 807, 864
  ice cream trucks, 830
  pets, 867
  safety, 268
  shoes, 536, 558
Chinese food, 542, 663
Cholesterol, 570, 571
Christians, 365
Christmas, 777
Christmas trees, 173, 174
Churches, 654
Cigarettes, 103, 161, 330, 331, 332
Circuitry, 473
Circulation, 304
Circumference, 483
Cities, 897, 898, 907
Citroëns, 869
City slickers, 400
Civil War, 17
Classical music, 163
Classrooms, 854
Cleaning, 51, 391, 769
Clergy, 183, 184, 185, 186, 187
Clerical staffs, 556
Closets, 623, 641

CLOTHING, 50, 109, 279, 377, 395, 420, 421, 544, 558, 623, 641, 643, 656, 668, 680, 785, 812, 892, 915, 927
Clout, 723
Cockroaches, 792, 838
Coffee, 93, 411, 646
Coins, 16, 564, 695, 924
Colds, 195
Collapse points, 125
Collections, record, 918
College
  bars, 467
  dormitories, 254
  medical school, 487
  memory, 488
  nostalgia, 444
  professors, 883
  recruiting, 879
  sidewalks, 346
  term papers, 425
  tuition, 270
Collisions, 427
COLOR, 59, 60, 61, 62, 86, 93, 109, 184, 318, 338, 396, 438, 510, 528, 572, 640, 671, 699, 753, 758, 759, 768, 773, 777, 788, 801, 886, 900
Complaints, 809, 810, 811
Compost, 846
Compromises, 301
Computers
  data storage, 632
  learning, 30, 361, 509, 612
  programming, 144, 145, 146, 147, 148, 513, 651, 676, 677, 760
  repair, 624
  systems, 258, 479, 625, 685, 828
  word processors, 603
Concrete, 787
Condominiums, 170, 171, 172, 666
Congress, 394
Construction, 314, 737, 822, 901
Consulting, 435
CONTAINERS, 58, 220, 243, 298, 300, 395, 434, 436, 476, 500, 548, 570, 574, 626, 665, 675, 690, 700, 745, 793, 846, 855, 871
Contests, 129, 474
Contra dancing, 513
Contracting, 822
CONVERSATIONS, 20, 21, 56, 74, 124, 138, 158, 193, 207, 265, 275, 284, 311, 357, 365, 376, 389, 413, 491, 568, 618, 645, 655, 691, 706, 711, 717, 723, 732, 782, 803, 818, 826, 829, 847, 852, 899
Cooking
  bread, 534, 744, 831
  chicken, 14, 484
  donuts, 290
  eggs, 12
  fish, 329
  frozen foods, 707
  hot fudge, 52

122

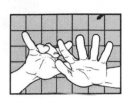